ADMIT YOU!

The Official Guide with Rankings, Proven Strategies and How You Too Will Get Accepted to the Best Private Day and Boarding Schools

ROSS D. BLANKENSHIP

ISBN: 1500181609
ISBN 13: 9781500181604
Library of Congress Control Number: 2014911242
CreateSpace Independent Publishing Platform
North Charleston, South Carolina

CONTENTS

ACKNOWLEDGEMENTS

I would like to thank the following people for making this possible and life that much greater:

Dr. D. Michael Blankenship, thank you for buying any book we ever needed and for telling us what we needed to hear—even if it was *sometimes* hard raising us as a single father. Though I'll never be able to save as many lives as you have, I hope to inspire as many people someday.

To my wife, Dr. Winslow Blankenship, the other doctor in my life: you provide infinite wisdom, care, and love, and I am blessed to have met you. Our daughter is a reflection of your beauty and smarts, all in one. Through your hard work, you inspire me to be a better person.

To my brother, Michael Blankenship, for being there anytime, every time. You're the best brother in the world.

And to five families who impacted my life: the Callaway family, Contratto family, Ghassabeh family, Browning family, and Byrne family. Each family believed, and that's all that matters.

I'm also beyond grateful to Josh Barr, who made this book happen.

Thank you as well to the Top Test Prep experts including Melissa Bojos (project leader) and our private and boarding school admissions team for continuing to help students get into the best schools!

This book is a journey, and our mission to *Admit You!* starts now.

INTRODUCTION

THE JOURNEY TO THE TOP

"Tell people what they need to hear, not what they want to hear."
—D. Michael Blankenship, MD

About one year ago, I sat at the conference table in our Top Test Prep offices in Washington, DC, looking out the window at the elite Sidwell Friends School across the street, and began contemplating ways to better educate more people about the admissions strategies and techniques we use to help students gain admission to top boarding and private day schools. For the past several years, we have helped thousands of students gain admission to the most elite schools. But what worked the most? How can other students get into top schools? How can you tell your son or daughter what's best when the process can be so vague and enigmatic? As a result I came up with this book title: *"Admit You!"*

The immediate goal was to eliminate the confusion many parents have about the admissions process and provide a definitive guide so that any child, anywhere in the world, would have the same opportunity. But the bigger goal was mission driven.

My mission is to help any student achieve her dream of getting into the best schools. Your son or daughter, or both, deserve the best.

I want this book to dispel the myths many parents and students have. You don't need a perfect SSAT score to get into Exeter. You don't need a perfect application to be admitted to Andover or Deerfield. The admissions officers want applications—with personal statements and supplemental questions—completed by the applicants and understand they will be looking at the work of someone not yet in high school.

Applicants and their parents tend to forget that there is a human component to the admissions process, with a real person at the other end of the tunnel reading their application.

Far too often, I have found myself in conversations with parents who perpetuate these myths and incorrect information. I wanted to shout from the mountaintop to eliminate much of the mystery that goes into applying to these great schools.

So I started sketching an outline for what this book might look like and discussed it with key members of the Top Test Prep staff.

All my life, I have rooted for the underdog. Despite growing up in Texarkana, Texas, three hours away from football-mad Dallas, I was the kid who would cheer for the lowly New Orleans Saints rather than the Dallas Cowboys. Now, I want all students and their parents who think they don't have a shot at getting into an elite school to read this book and realize they can do it, if they apply themselves.

Furthermore, I know the importance of going to a great school. Growing up in a small town on the Arkansas border, I had many more opportunities than my former classmates just because I attended boarding school. That is not to say that a public school cannot provide the same opportunities, but by surrounding students with a high concentration of talented classmates, private and boarding schools put their enrollment in a better situation to challenge themselves and each other. You are only as great as the people around you! Both your network and who you know matter.

Admit You! is your road map to gaining admission to your dream school. I will share many of Top Test Prep's tried and true strategies with you and walk you through the application process, from your first campus tour to sending in your deposit check. You will learn about the Hawk, the Scout, and the Veteran, as well as all of the mistakes most of the applicants make. Follow my advice, and you are sure to stand out. Yes, this advice will sometimes be hard to hear and counterintuitive. In fact, parents often want to think their kid is perfect, no matter what the circumstance. However, my goal is to tell you what you need to hear and not just what you want to hear. After all, the truth will set you free and help you on the path to admission to the best schools in America.

The application process has changed greatly in recent years. One consultation with a family that was out of touch sticks out in my mind. The family flew to Washington, DC, to meet with me, eager to get their son into a top boarding school. The mother walked in toting her Hermès handbag, Gucci glasses, and Louis Vuitton accessories. It was as if she walked right off the set of *Legally Blonde,* the comedy where a sorority girl, played by Reese Witherspoon, attends Harvard Law School.

She sat down in my office and said, "How much am I going to have to pay to get my kid into Trinity School or Horace Mann in New York City?"

Whoa! I explained to her that these schools already have plenty of money—Trinity School and Horace Mann both have endowments in the hundreds of millions of dollars. And while I'm sure a few million more wouldn't hurt, schools such as Trinity School are most interested in bringing in talented students. Money will take you far in life, but the old-boy network is not the same, and you cannot buy your way into schools. That's not what admissions are about these days. Even if you have money, students must find their voice and show their passion. There is no person who can be guaranteed admission without following the tips and strategies we use in this book.

I write to you as an admissions insider, some say the "the best admissions expert in America"—but most importantly as a parent, too.

I am confident that if you read this book, follow our tips, and practice with our test-prep strategies, the best schools will...*Admit You!*

Let's get started.
Ross D. Blankenship
TopTestPrep.com | Chairman

———

Warning: This book will help you get into the best private schools in America.

It's up to you what you do at your dream school once you get in.

If you agree or disagree with anything in the book or if you just need help, call us at 800-501-7737.

CHAPTER 1

THE HUMAN ELEMENT

So you want to go to private school: boarding school—perhaps even one of the nation's most prestigious schools, such as Exeter or Andover—or a top private day school, such as Trinity.

You have seen the rankings and checked out several schools' websites.

Maybe you are way ahead of the game and have the applications in front of you.

Or maybe you are a parent and want to send your son or daughter to one of these schools because—as I agree—you think it is the best way for them to get ahead, even at this early age.

But then you look over the application, and once you get past the basics, it looks daunting. Personal statements? Essays? Supplemental materials? Seriously, what seventh or eighth grader has an authentic résumé—not merely some bloated story full of puffed up sort-of experiences that are not realistic for someone so young—that will make them stand apart?

That's where this book comes in.

Admit You! is your map to mastering the application process.

Why should you listen to me?

I once was in your shoes, and looking back, there is no question that even though I was ahead of most of my peers, I was still completely clueless about the process. Heck, when my brother and I applied to some of the country's elite boarding schools, we were just a pair of teenagers from Texarkana, Texas, whose only knowledge on the subject came from a (likely outdated) fourteen-dollar guidebook I had bought at the local bookstore—certainly the only one on the shelf in the store in my neck of the woods.

I can still remember when I arrived at Northfield Mount Hermon School (NMH) in rural north central Massachusetts. I stepped off the airport shuttle onto a sprawling campus with my ostrich cowboy boots and ten-gallon George Strait hat and was a total misfit with nothing in common with my pink-haired roommate from New Hampshire.

While I certainly was homesick and uncomfortable until my second year at NMH, I soon found my way. I grew to love the school and be a part of the community. My "work job" at NMH—which every student was required to have, and, yes, I know it sounds like a double negative—was to be a campus tour guide. It did not take long for me to realize which applicants were more likely to be accepted and which were bound for the "waitlist" or "rejected" piles. I usually could make the call less than halfway through each tour!

My interest in the admissions process continued at Cornell University, where I was elected to the Educational Policy Committee and served on the Academic Integrity Hearing Board. And now, in my work at Top Test Prep, I continue to read college applications and help hundreds of students navigate the college and high school admissions process.

All told, I have probably read close to five thousand applications for colleges and elite private and boarding schools. Parents, I have led campus tours for your children and even given tours to people like Robert Reich, former secretary of labor under President Clinton, when his son was applying to NMH. I know how to guide you through this challenging process and help you make a positive impression while avoiding the common pitfalls that even the most knowledgeable parents and students often make without even realizing.

Admit You! is not going to automatically secure your spot at Phillips Andover or Deerfield Academy. Heck, it might not get you into any of the schools on our Top Ten Boarding Schools in America or Top Ten Private Day Schools in America. Our book is not going to turn your 3.0 grade point average into a 3.97 with your only one and only B coming after you missed two weeks of classes because of a rare blood disorder. It will not take your 35th percentile on your third attempt at taking the SSAT and suddenly make it to the 95th percentile.

By reading this book, taking the time to let the material seep in, and following our advice, you can improve your chances of getting into the school you want, and no doubt you will be a much more attractive admissions candidate than other students with similar profiles.

———

What are the most common mistakes made in the private and boarding school admissions process?

You will never believe it because it seems so simple.

Too many students, or their parents, fail to remember that real people are reading their application. Even if their application is filled out online, actual living, breathing people are on the other end, deciding whether the applicant is a great fit for the school. There is a human element to the admissions process—and you need to know who is reading your application and what things they are looking for in the few moments that you have their attention.

Crazy, right?

Far too often, applications read as if they are written for a robot, not someone with the ability to discern between what is written into an application and cold, hard reality.

So who are the people who work in admissions offices? They generally fall into one of three categories.

1. *The greeter/administrative helper—the Hawk*: This is usually the first person to come into contact with your application and might seem like a receptionist when you arrive on campus for an interview. The Hawk might actually be one of the most important people in the whole admissions process, as she gazes intently upon every applicant's file and any interviewee walking into

her "home." Bottom line: Don't underestimate this person like so many of your fellow applicants do!

2. *The junior representative—the Scout*: This person is likely to be between twenty-five and thirty-five years old. There is a good chance the Scout is an alumnus of the school. Maybe now this person has returned to her alma mater and teaches a class or two or, more likely, coaches a sport. Each Scout is responsible for a specific geographic area.

3. *The senior admissions officer—the Veteran*: This person is an admissions veteran and knows the process inside and out. She also has the final say if there is any question about an application and quite possibly also serves as the school's financial aid officer. More likely than not, however, this person serves as a mentor to the others in the admissions office and gets those people to start

thinking like they do—which means they all generally agree on whether to offer admission to a candidate.

It is vital to know that these are the three types of people who will come in contact with your application.

Try to look at the process through their eyes. Imagine that they see hundreds or perhaps thousands of applications each year. And nearly all of these applicants have high test scores. They have great grade point averages. They play sports and participate in other extracurricular activities. They come from powerful families. They have parents who are CEOs of national and international companies. These are kids who studied the piano before they knew the ABCs and who were bilingual before age ten. They are overachieving, privileged, and well-traveled children.

So how can you stand out—especially if you're just a hard-working student from the suburbs without high-powered credentials like these?

Keep in mind the Hawk, the Scout, and the Veteran.
They know the campus. They know the student body. They have a general idea of who will fit in and contribute to the school and which students are just going through the process because their moms or dads want them to or their grandparents went to a certain school. Their job is to screen people and make sure they can add value to the campus life.

Most applicants never think about this. They think that with a high SSAT or ISEE score, they will get accepted. It's a binary perception. *And it is dead wrong!*

Admissions officers don't just sit in their office and review applications nonstop. It's not like the paperwork comes in year-round. These people are fully part of the campus and day-to-day life there. Their job is to screen applicants and make sure they can add value to campus life, whether it is through diversity, sports, academics, extracurricular activities, or any other manner.

The human element of private and boarding school admissions is so palpable. If you're going to be there every single day, how do you fit in or contribute? Most people don't realize the layers.

Look at me. Here I was, Ross Blankenship, a lanky, awkward eighth grader. I was already more than six feet tall and a head taller than nearly all of my peers. I was probably the only person from Texarkana ever to apply to most of these schools, which I thought would get the door opened slightly. Still, I recognized that to be admitted to one of these top schools, I had to stand out in other ways than just being from an interesting town. I knew there was more to it. I knew I had to conquer the SSAT because maybe they wouldn't think someone from my part of the country, where these exams are not popular, would score well. My brother and I traveled two hours to Little Rock to take the exam, and even then, we were the only ones taking it that day! I knew my grades were going to enter into the decision—but how much would they matter? It's not like these elite boarding school admissions officers were going to see my application and think to themselves, *Wow! That guy mastered the Texarkana Independent School District. We've got to have him!* I also knew I couldn't write a boring essay. I had to have a bit of spunk or creativity and make sure admissions officers got to know me. I like to think of admissions as a multidimensional process—not just what is on paper, but how it can come alive. I don't think students and their parents realize there are more parts to it than test scores.

What's another thing students and their parents don't realize?

When you arrive at an admissions office for a school visit, the secretary or administrative assistant—the Hawk—is checking you out from the moment you walk in the door. The Hawk is looking at how the student comports herself—and how parents act as well. *Is the student interested? Or is the parent telling the student how to act? How did the student dress? How does she sit? Does she look bored? Is she looking around the office, trying to imagine herself attending this school? Is the student on her cell phone?*

I can still vividly remember one of my first days as a tour guide at NMH. As with most boarding schools, each tour I gave was just for one family. This time, I was leading a family from California around the 215-acre campus, and the parents kept telling their son that he needed to tell the admissions officers what they wanted to hear about the school. The kid clearly didn't feel comfortable. The parent was coaching the whole way. I went back and offered my opinion: I didn't know if the student would be happy here. Needless to say, the kid did not end up at NMH.

That brings me to another important tip: leave the cell phone in your car!

Nothing screams "I'm not that interested" more than an applicant who is e-mailing, texting, or scanning Facebook in the minutes leading up to this important interview. Don't just put your phone on vibrate or silent when it's your big moment to meet with the admissions officer. Don't even be tempted to look at your phone just to check the time. Don't bring it with you at all!

Another tip: introduce yourself to the Hawk.

How many of your peers are doing this? Not that many, right? And when you follow up with a handwritten thank-you to the Scout or the Veteran for interviewing you, send another to the Hawk. Trust me. This person has a keen idea of how things run and what applicants will be successful, and she gets involved in the admissions conversation.

Yet one more tip.

Ask open-ended questions of the Hawk. *What does this person like the most about the campus?* This is your opportunity to stand out—and one that way too many applicants miss out on. They don't realize this is somebody who not only checks you in, but also checks you out!

You have to remember: when you walk into that admissions office, you are walking into somebody's house! (And yes, it often is a house.) The Hawk sees the parents telling their children to sit up straight, show better posture, or stop chewing gum. I've seen it happen, and I know the immediate negative impression that it makes. The Hawk sees this going on and thinks the student is not there on her own volition and that the parent is dictating that the student go on this interview. If you have five applications of similar quality, guess which is the first one not making the cut, just based on the five minutes the student spent sitting in a waiting area?

As ridiculous as this might sound, that is the way it goes. Don't become one of the waiting room casualties!

Yes, to some extent, when you are twelve or thirteen or fourteen years old, you might need to be told how to dress and look sharp and present yourself. But once you walk in the front door of the admissions office, it's about you and how you connect. If it doesn't look like you own what is happening, you're in trouble. You need to look comfortable—don't dress over the top or too shabby. For boys a sport coat and khakis are fine, and a tie is optional. For girls pants and a blouse or a dress are good. No sneakers! You don't want to be fighting your clothing. Your dress should reflect who you are. Children this age don't dress up that often. If you get to a point where you are uncomfortable in your clothing, you are going to be distracted.

Remember, you are walking into somebody's house, into somebody's environment, and you want to be a part of the family. When you walk into a family reunion, are you walking in stiff, or are you friendly and casual?

It is important for parents to make sure their children can focus on the main task at hand. In an effort to remain focused, not get distracted, and perhaps even provide a familiar conversation topic, I usually suggest students take along a book that they especially enjoy. Let the admissions officers see it, and explain what you like about this book.

> Myth: Admissions officers are machines. They just go through their checklist, and if your application meets enough of the requirements, you will be admitted.
>
> Fact: Admissions officers are people too, with real feelings and emotions. Having the grades and test scores does not guarantee admission, just as lower grades and lower test scores will not disqualify an applicant.

The next mistake that too many people make: they ask the wrong questions.

Think about it this way. By the time you arrive on campus for an interview, you should be well versed in what a school has to offer and its strengths. Don't ask the St. Paul's admissions officer how many of St. Paul's students get into Ivy League schools. Don't ask the folks at Groton in what percentile you need to score on the SSAT in order to be considered for admission or how many AP courses the school offers. A) You should know these figures (or at least estimates) before you interview, so already you're off on the wrong foot, showing you have not done your homework and you have a general lack of interest. B) Think about the answers these questions will elicit. Will they provoke conversation and discussion, or will they get a brief, terse reply? These are boring questions that can hurt applicants.

In addition to doing some preparation before the campus visit and interview, **I have one other suggestion**: when you get to campus, walk around and take an un-guided tour. Try to get a feel for the campus and picture how you belong. Yes, you've looked at a school's website ad nauseam, but this is a chance to see what things are like. *How much space is devoted to different interests? Is the hockey rink the nicest building on campus with the capacity to seat three times the student body?* Go to the campus-life building, look at the bulletin board, and scan the volunteer opportunities or extracurricular activities on campus. By the time you get to the admissions office, you should have a good sense of the school's mission and be able to discuss the school in a candid way. Trust me; if you walk into the admissions office and ask a question about the service club that meets the third Saturday morning of each month, it will be noticed.

Alas, most people see the interview as an opportunity to show off. They are going to walk in and tell everything about themselves and their lives and how great they are. But admissions officers want to hear you ask questions that show interest about a school. *Wow, the hockey rink is big, and it's my favorite sport to watch. Do most of the students attend games, and is this a source of school spirit?* Note that this somewhat violates my theory of sticking to open-ended questions, but I think that the interest it shows in a particular school outweighs the drawbacks of asking a question with a definitive answer.

Also, put yourself in the place of the admissions officer. What would be going through your head while you are stuck listening to a thirteen-year-old rattle off her "life experiences" as you silently nod along? Would you believe each of these middle school students has accomplished so many impressive things at such a young age? Of course not!

Instead, start the discussion flowing. Ask the admissions officers how they ended up in their positions. Ask about the student body. Be ready and willing to think on your feet and go with the flow. Be flexible with your follow-up questions—don't stick to a script and simply go down the list checking off boxes! **Never stick with the script!** And don't get cute. If someone asks, "What's your favorite book?" don't reply, "Well, what's your favorite book?" If you want to get that promotion or get that spot in next year's freshman class, you have to act or think like people already there.

Again, you only have a certain amount of time to impress the admissions staff. Choosing a theme and knowing yourself is incredibly important, as is being able to get that message across. And parents, coaching is OK—heck, it's expected. Help your child find her voice and confidence. But this needs to happen before you walk in the front door.

––––––

Now that we've gotten you inside the admissions office door, **what score do you need on the SSAT or ISEE in order to be considered?**

If your goal is to attend one of the schools on our top-ten lists, you should have a score in the top 10th percentile.

Does this mean you absolutely must be in the top 10 percent? Of course not. There are always exceptions. Heck, my brother and I did not even apply to boarding schools until after the application deadline, and we matriculated to elite schools! But if you want to have the best possible chance and make this wish come true, you need to score well.

Your test scores won't guarantee you a slot in a freshman class, but a low score can hurt your chances.

If you don't score well the first time you take the SSAT or ISEE, you can take it again, but I recommend never taking any test more than twice. (*Note: you can only take the ISEE once every six months. More on that in Chapter 5.*) Also, even if it is your first time taking the SSAT or ISEE, go in with the mind-set that you will only take the test once. If, in the back of your head, you tell yourself that you might retake the test, you will not perform as well.

So is the application just a numbers game?

Absolutely not. It's much more than numbers. It's a holistic picture of the student. Seeing if the student is going to fit in. Seeing if the student is going to add value to the campus. If it were only about the scores, schools would not fill up. Some students are better at math or writing or English, and there are only so many top 10 percenters to go around.

But if you are not in the top 10th percentile, perhaps it is time to reconsider your list. That's not to say you cannot or should not apply to the schools on our top-ten lists. If that's where you want you to go, by all means do your best and go for it, follow my recommendations, and hit the throttle, full speed ahead. But you should have realistic expectations; shooting for the moon is great, but we don't want anyone to be disappointed at the end of the process.

> Myth: An applicant's grades and SSAT or ISEE score are the only things that matter.
>
> Fact: Each application is judged in so many ways. So many applicants tout great grades and test scores that the best way to stand out is by showing passion and making a personal connection with the admissions officers.

Should you submit supplemental materials, such as a voice recording or art portfolio?

Maybe.

What kind of wishy-washy answer is that, you want to know?

Well, if the supplemental materials are exceptional, by all means send them in a bright package with a bow or ribbon on top! But if these items are not exceptional, then don't clog up the application process. The last thing an admissions officer wants to do is listen to a thirteen-year-old sing off-key as she plays the guitar haphazardly.

Or you could do what one of our clients did as she made her campus visits. Stacy was an exceptional piano player. In the middle of her tour to Phillips Exeter Academy, as they went through the music building, Stacy sat down at a piano and started playing. It worked like a charm! You could envision her as an Exeter student. The tour guide went back and told the admissions officers, and it stood out. As an eighth grader, she was incredible. Don't submit your supplemental materials just to do it or because you can. This is where parents are needed. Too often, parents say what a kid wants to hear, not what they need to hear. Don't try to make your kid something they are not. Supplemental materials can help, but only if there is mastery above their age level.

———

Should you apply to a day school or a boarding school?

This is a tricky question and, obviously, is up to each individual. Personally, I think a boarding school provides the best preparation for college. The question, though, is whether a student has the maturity level to go off on their own at such a young age and be successful. At its core a boarding school is a college environment, and you are living a collegiate experience before you get to college.

Fundamentally, there is not a significant difference between day schools and boarding schools. The curricula are similar. You generally will be surrounded by brilliant classmates and learn from great teachers.

The key question is whether you are the type of student who can leave home at this age and thrive in a boarding school environment. Usually, this is a student who has sought out the academic or extracurricular activity as opposed to the student whose parent is the driving force. This is a student who seeks out opportunities on her own, rather than waiting for someone else to suggest it. It might be 1 percent of the population that is prepared for this.

It is not easy for a young teenager to make this move, and it takes some courage. You are in that puberty maturation phase and already worried about what people think of you and how they look at you. You have to be able to overcome that.

When you attend boarding school, class and campus life blend together. NMH was my life. It's not just wearing a jersey or letter jacket or vest. There's nothing wrong with day schools, but boarding schools become your identity. When you live there and don't leave at three or five o'clock and instead go to your dorm room and eat all your meals together and hear "Lights out" at nine thirty every night, it is pretty intense.

———

What about applying as a tenth grader?

If you are applying to boarding school, I believe you should apply earlier rather than later. Boarding school campuses are a way of life. Once students begin living together, they get to know each other's routines and form friendships. The later you enroll, the harder it is to find your place on campus. Think of it as moving to a new city and sending your kids to a new school. It is easier for your kids to adapt if they arrive at a new school at the same time everyone else does.

Of course, that is not to say it can't be done. Look at my older brother, Michael. While I went to NMH as a freshman, he entered Exeter as a junior and had no problem assimilating. But he also wrestled, was on the crew team, and played intramural hockey. He got involved quickly. And he was mature for his age—that helped, too.

———

What about international students?

More and more students are coming from countries like China, South Korea, Japan, and even South America. It is getting harder and harder for students from those places to set themselves apart. Think of what it might have been like if ten of my classmates from Texarkana—which might as well be a foreign nation for the schools on our top-ten lists—had applied to NMH. Obviously, the more unique your applications, the better off you are—provided what makes you stand out is legitimate and not contrived.

For individuals from these countries that are sending more students to boarding schools, testing is not always going to get them in. Their ability to speak English and communicate in this language becomes crucial. Admissions officers know this can be an impediment—both to a student's ability to contribute on campus and to the student's happiness. Schools do not want unhappy students who are more prone to leaving before graduation.

Admissions officers are always on the lookout to see how foreign students immerse themselves. Does a Korean applicant only have interest in other Korean students during her visit? The campus has to become a melting pot of different cultures; schools do not want cliques to form.

———

About one thousand middle school students per year come through the doors of Top Test Prep. Of this group, roughly 10 percent are vocal about the process and have a maturity level that distinguishes them from the applicant pool. The other 90 percent? It's not that they are dummies—almost all are capable of putting in the time and effort—but usually they have been coerced and prodded into being there to talk to our staff, as opposed to wanting to be there themselves.

You know how we find out the truth?

We sit down first with Mom and Dad and the student, but then we ask the parent to leave the room. That's where the truth comes out, and candor becomes part of the conversation.

I ask them open-ended, "What do you feel about this whole thing?" It leaves them the opportunity to say they're not sure about it or maybe there are some good opportunities. I have to separate and figure out how motivated they are themselves. My guidance through the application process can only help so much; it works much better if a student buys in and is motivated.

Sometimes that motivation comes from pointing out the opportunities that are out there. Let's say a student is an athlete and you point out the available facilities. Or there is a wonderful music building available 24-7 for the blossoming pianist. That's when it comes alive for them. Most public school campuses are one building, and everything is bunched together with bigger classrooms. A piano in the music lobby? Ha! And not one student comes to our office uninterested in smaller classes.

So 10 percent is motivated and gung ho. The other 90 percent, I point out the opportunities, and it changes the whole dynamic for almost all of them. Be aware, you have an audience of kids, and they have tight friendships and best buddies they've done everything with. With private day schools, this is less of an issue;

but with boarding schools, you're uprooting the student and putting her in a new environment.

There is one last thing to always remember: don't be a phony.

Whatever you say or do, make sure it is genuine. From my Top Test Prep office, I can look across the street and see Sidwell Friends School, one of the nation's elite day schools, in Washington, DC, whose alumni include Chelsea Clinton and whose current students include Sasha and Malia Obama. Do you think the folks at Sidwell are laughing inside when kids of ultraconservatives nearly always sneak in a mention of President Obama during their campus visits?

What's the takeaway?

Name-dropping, being a phony, and not sticking true to who you are can damage your chances for admission. The Hawk, the Scout, and the Veteran are savvy people who know this process inside and out and can quickly spot who belongs and who does not. Don't be predictable. There are plenty of students from well-off and well-known families, but a shortage of those who genuinely present themselves as self-motivated. That is how one kid made his way from Texarkana to NMH.

Myth: The application deadline is hard and fast. If you decide too late to apply to a school, you can forget about it.

Fact: While it is by far best to meet the application deadline, you can still apply after the fact, but know that you will have to explain this to the admissions officers.

CHAPTER 2

TAKE OWNERSHIP OF YOUR APPLICATIONS

Now that you have an inside view of the admissions process, what should you do next? Already we have seen the importance of being prepared and doing our homework, so let's keep that going.

In a nutshell here is my suggested timeline to put yourself in the best position to gain admission to the school of your choice:

- As soon as you begin thinking about a private or boarding school, get the application for the current school year for that school.

- May–June–July
  - Contact schools. They will start a file on you, and you should create a file for each school in which you are interested.
  - Approach people you will be asking for recommendations, and let them know what you will need from them.
  - Start preparing for the SSAT or ISEE.
  - Become familiar with the Gateway to Prep Schools website.

- August–September–October
  - Get the new applications that you will fill out for the upcoming school year.
  - Schedule your campus visits and interviews.
  - Take the SSAT or ISEE.
  - Sit down with your recommenders and make sure they have all the material and information they need.

- November–December:
  - Visit the campuses to which you are applying, and interview with admissions officers.
  - Write personal statements and essays *after* your visits.
  - Refine applications so that everything is complete.

- January:
  - Send applications, and enroll in the fall!

Looking over this timeline, it sounds simple. If you stick to the schedule, it will be. But know this is a time-consuming process that requires an honest effort. Following these steps keeps you ahead of the curve and puts you on the road to enrolling in your private or boarding school.

Parent tip: From the beginning, strive to get your son or daughter to take ownership of the application process. It might not be easy. Few students this age are ready to take this charge. But the sooner your children buy in, the better off they will be while your guiding hand steers the process. You might have to poke and prod. You might have to issue a few reminders or do a little nagging. Trust me that this is worth the effort and any short-term struggle. When your child is the driving force in the application process, it makes a positive impression on admissions officers who perceive this applicant as a go-getter. Try your best to avoid picking the schools, finding the websites, locating the applications, and printing them out. By putting the onus on your child, you avoid your son or daughter relying on you because they believe you will finish the job if they do not.

The application process should start as soon as you have an inkling that private or boarding school interests you.

March–April–May

♦ **Get the current applications for the schools in which you are interested.** The applications will differ from year to year, so this will not be the same application you fill out, but reading this will help you know what to expect. The more familiar you are with what an application requires, particularly the essay questions and personal statements, the better prepared you will be to fill out your own applications. This is a great opportunity for parents and children to work together. When reading the applications, figure out which applications will require more time than others so that if you apply to one of these schools, you can budget your time appropriately. Also, note what essay questions are being asked and discuss potential ways to address these questions. Create a list of schools and figure out which ones you find most interesting so you can focus your attention on these schools. Although I recommend parents try to get their children to assume responsibility for the application process, parents should keep in mind that younger students will need more guidance.

♦ **Develop a list of schools in which you are interested, and contact each admissions office.** Students, you want to let the admissions officers of each school know you exist as a potential applicant. Many schools have a quick questionnaire online for each potential applicant to complete. I also recommend making a phone call, which is more personal than an e-mail or letter. Every little bit that helps you stand out is important! After you reach out, each school will start a file on you. And you should keep a file on each school. Take notes on whom you speak with from the office, questions they ask, and how the call goes—you can reference this in future conversations. Ask to be sent the application for the following school year as soon as it becomes available. Keep in mind that as soon as you reach out, the admissions office is starting to make similar notes on you—gauging your interest and seeing how you might fit in as a student at the school. They also might take a look at your social-media footprint, so be careful not to have anything that could be damaging on your Facebook, Twitter, or Instagram pages.

♦ **Notify anyone who you plan to ask for a recommendation so they can prepare.** The best recommendation letters are not written overnight. They take time. You do not want to annoy a recommender by asking for a rush job—it will show in their work, and their recommendation will not be as personalized! This is another good time for parents and children to work together. Discuss potential recommenders: Who knows the student best and will be able to provide her perspective for an admissions office? Was there a particular teacher or two who engaged the student the most? The parent and child should schedule a short appointment with every person being asked for a recommendation and make sure they are comfortable writing the recommendation. Don't assume that the history teacher with whom you believe you have a good relationship already knows you well enough to nail your recommendation letter. The Hawk, the Scout, and the Veteran read hundreds of these letters each year and know which recommendations are genuine.

♦ **Start your SSAT and ISEE preparation.** Just like becoming familiar with applications, the sooner a student becomes familiar with whichever test they plan to take, the better they will score. Buy a book with practice tests. Take a prep class if you have the ability. Even though the students are younger, they should treat these tests in the same manner in which high school students look at the SAT and ACT. Parents, have an honest conversation with your child regarding the standardized tests and what they need to do in order to prepare. Students might be resistant to studying for another test. It is your job to motivate them.

- ◆ **Map out a schedule.** Create a master calendar that includes the deadlines for all applications as well as a checklist for what each application requires. I cannot overstate the importance of being organized. You do not want to be searching at the last minute for a recommendation letter from your child's English or math teachers that some schools require. Become familiar with the Gateway to Prep Schools website, where nearly fifty elite schools have come together to make it easier for applicants to obtain information and apply. There even is a group application, similar to the Common Application that many colleges and universities accept.

Myth: A parent should fill out the application for admission because they will do it best.

Fact: The parents should stay out of the way and merely provide guidance after the student has filled out the application to the best of her abilities. By having the student fill out the application, she demonstrates an interest in gaining admission and eliminates the potential for their application to be inauthentic.

August–September–October

In the fall you are ready to get down to business. You get each application. Check in with your recommenders to make sure they have all the information they need, are on schedule, and know your deadlines. I advise having recommendations in hand well in advance. Take the ISEE or SSAT. Schedule your campus visits and interviews. By doing these things ahead of time, you are showing schools that you are proactive and serious about matriculating. You want to be seen as someone eager to gain admission, not someone just going through the process.

By lining up these things and setting your timeline, you put yourself in the best possible position to gain admission to the school you want to attend. Maybe you struggle with a particular essay question. Maybe you don't like the recommendation letter from your math teacher and want to go over it with her and discuss any

TAKE OWNERSHIP OF YOUR APPLICATIONS

potential changes. Maybe you get a 1950 on the SSAT and know you can do better. Remember Stacy, the pianist? She got a 1900 on her first try on the SSAT as she had done little preparation and lacked confidence because she had not even taken a practice test. But she was motivated and took ownership; with the help of Top Test Prep, we got her to the high 2300s. She got in everywhere she applied, including Andover, Exeter, and St. Paul's!

> **Parent tip:** If your child does not seem interested in attending private or boarding school and is not motivated, this is a good time for a pep talk. Every year at Top Test Prep, I counsel plenty of families where the parents want this to happen but the kids initially balk at the process. After all, most of their friends are not doing the "work" of the application process, so why should they have to do this? This is quite normal for students this age; it does not mean your child is not open to the idea. Look at it another way: no student is against going on a trip to visit some cool schools and meet some students. It's not the mandatory Disneyland trip—it's a new adventure! Few kids will say, "I don't want to go check this out." There is an openness to it. Whatever the case, if any student stays on my suggested schedule of starting to prepare as early as possible and then works through the summer and fall to complete her applications, there is plenty of time to adjust for any possible setbacks or delays. If your child is hesitant, talk with her. Find out specifically what your child dislikes about the idea of going to a better school. If she is worried about losing friends or having to fit into a new school, assuage your child's concerns. Visiting the school will excite your child, but you need to ensure your child remains motivated throughout the application process.

One of the biggest problems I see every year is the family that rushes through everything over the Christmas holidays. (Notice that I say family here, because in this instance it is the parents doing much of the work!) I'll never forget one student who came to us a few years ago. Not only did James and his family wait until literally the last minute, James was applying to the best of Top Test Prep's top ten boarding schools. Those schools know the earlier your application is received, the more organized you are and the stronger you feel about matriculating. James had scored in the 99th percentile on the SSAT! His grades were strong. But he and his parents just rushed the whole process, and it showed. His essays read like rough drafts. His recommendations seemed impersonal. His brag sheet sounded like a laundry list of items that were not realistic. He got into one out of ten schools and ended up deciding to apply for the following school year.

Does that mean you are doomed to fail if you don't follow my suggested timeline? Of course not. There are always exceptions. Look at my example: my brother and I did not even apply until after the application deadlines. But we found our own narrative and explained why we were so late in the process. It worked! Can you imagine how it would sound if James did this? "Well, I was too lazy to get things done sooner and make a solid effort because I knew that Mom and Dad would take care of it for me." How would that go over?

Do not give up if you are a seventh or eighth grader reading this book over Christmas break. You can still apply, but be realistic about setting goals. Map out the process because it will take three months. **My goal for this book is both to enlighten you about the benefits of these schools and also to inform you about the process.** And be candid when inevitably you are asked the question, "Well, why are you so late to apply?" Be honest with your reply: "I was not considering boarding school as an option, but I changed my mind, and this is something I want to do."

The average application, not including the writing samples, will take you ten hours total to complete. Much of the demographic information and data is the same on all applications; for the schools that participate in the Gateway to Prep Schools, you can save time by filling out the Candidate Profile. For other schools, take your time and be sure to read each line carefully before filling it out. The supplemental essays will differ from application to application, and your personal statement should be different from school to school as well. **Your essays and personal statements should not be written until after visiting each campus.** Again, if you are just going through the motions and sending the same application to multiple schools, the Hawk, the Scout, and the Veteran will notice. **If a school thinks you are doing the same thing on every application, it kills you!** It destroys your chances. They do not want to feel as though they are second best. You should go out of your way to make each school feel like it is its first choice. Think about it: Many of these schools are selective and note that they admit only a small percentage of those who apply. They are more likely to admit a candidate they are certain will matriculate in order to maintain this prestigious selectivity.

Myth: The application seems easy. It should only take a few minutes to fill out.

Fact: On average, each application should take ten hours to complete. All applications are not the same, nor should your personal statements and supplemental essays be the same from one application to the next.

Parent tip: It is vital for students to fill out the application to the best of their own abilities. They might not know everything and need some help, but the students should give it their best shot first. Then parents can step in and help polish. Guess what? If the student stops thinking this is their process, they are going to do the same thing when it comes to the SSAT or ISEE and think their parents are going to give them the answers!

*** Filling Out Your Application ***

This brings me to **three of the biggest mistakes** made in the application process:

1. The parent does every single thing. Which, of course, leads to...

2. The student takes no ownership. She does not even take the time to visit a school website or Facebook page because of the knowledge that Mom or Dad will swoop in to the rescue and take care of everything.

3. Students come off as inauthentic. Part of this mistake is overstating their activities. They list thirty extracurricular activities when the reality is if you are in sixth or seventh or eighth grade, there is no chance that you have the time to be so involved and make an impact in so many interests. The best way to stand out is not with a large number of things you have done, but by showing the things you have done about which you are **passionate**. Passion is defined here as the person, place, subject, event, or thing that inspires you and moves you to take a leadership role in some area of your life. Ask yourself what you are passionate about and why, and convey this. Your application should be a window for admissions officers to get to know you.

Going back to my time as a student tour guide at NMH School, I remember overhearing the admissions officers often talk about the fact that a student was different in person than she appeared on the application. Why? Because the student—or, more likely, her parents—projected one thing on paper and another in her interview and campus visit. This candidate is almost never getting accepted! "Who was this guy?" I can recall the Scout saying one time. "He had written this epic sonnet in his application, but when he came here, he was mundane and uninspiring." Time and again this happens. Don't be this person! Be authentic, complete the application yourself, and, as we learned in Chapter 1, remember that admissions officers are people, too. Compel them to accept you. They look at hundreds of applications each year and can spot a phony from a mile away! You must write the personal statements and supplemental essays and be prepared to talk about your writing when you interview. What you put in your application should mirror how you appear when you visit the campus. In other words, **what you put on paper has to reflect who you are as a person**!

Remember that assignment you had in third grade called show-and-tell? You brought your favorite toy to school so you could talk about how it was the coolest thing you had ever owned. Everyone in the class was impressed, and by the end of the presentation, everyone wanted your toy. This is what students need to do with their application: use the application to **show what they have done** and **tell admissions officers about it** as opposed to just bragging about their accomplishments and interests. That is a critical element that most students miss.

Myth: List every activity in which you have participated. You need to show the admissions officers that you are well rounded.

Fact: Quality is better than quantity. Instead of mentioning the wide array of items in which you are involved, focus on one or two and demonstrate your passion for those items.

November–December

By November and December, you have completed much of each application and thought about your essay topics. You are completing your campus visits. Now it is time to start writing your essays and personal statements. At some point during this step, think about your campus visit and interview to each school and see if there is a point to reference something that stood out from that day.

Completing the essays and personal statements should take one to two weeks each. Budget time for several sittings of thirty to forty-five minutes, going through and rewriting each piece several times. The first session should be free writing—don't worry about edits or revisions. Just start getting your thoughts down, and let the ideas flow.

Essay tip 1: Pick a topic for which you are passionate. It can be a hobby you enjoy in your free time or a subject you enjoy at school—something that fires you up!

Selecting the right topic ensures that you have plenty of thoughts to share and sets up your writing to be personal and convey emotion. Be sure to set aside this time and concentrate on your writing—this focus will show up in the final product. Each time you sit down, the work should improve. If this is not happening, consult a parent, teacher, or other adult, and find a way to make this happen.

Essay tip 2: Do *not* write about saving the world—especially those students who come from money or means and think they have to be viewed as sympathetic to the plight of others. I have seen too many applications where students want to help the homeless or end world hunger. Let's stop that nonsense! Admissions officers are bored with it! It is rarely authentic. Be yourself. Don't try to be a savior. Try to be somebody who is passionate about a subject, and share those feelings with the admissions officers who read your application. Save the world on your own time. Seriously, 15 to 20 percent of applicants write one of these essays. Admissions officers have been known to openly curse their proliferation. Even if you believe this, do not write it in your personal statement. Talk about it in your interview if you must.

Essay tip 3: Read your essay out loud to at least one other person. Take your time while reading. If something does not sound right, change it. Put yourself in the position of the admissions officers, who are reading hundreds of applications. When they come across an application that is easy to read and allows them to picture a candidate and her emotion and passion, it makes a positive impression.

———

January

While the application deadline for most schools is not until mid-January or early February **do not** wait until the last possible moment to send yours in. Do not ask whether your application has to be received or only postmarked by the deadline! This shows a lack of interest on your part in making things happen. Schools have plenty of other applications from which to choose. Do not give the Hawk, the Scout, or the Veteran any reason to mark you down. Your applications should be finished by January! By taking the initiative and staying ahead of the game, you are demonstrating an interest in being an active participant at your new school.

CHAPTER 3

THE OFFICIAL RANKINGS, AND WHY THEY MATTER

Let me preface this chapter by saying there are hundreds of boarding schools and private day schools across the country. There is a place that is perfect for every student.

In this book we will focus on the nation's elite schools—Top Test Prep's Top Ten Boarding Schools and Top Test Prep's Top Ten Private Day Schools. Maybe you are not interested in schools on this list—does that mean *Admit You!* (this book) is not for you?

Nothing could be further from the truth.

This book is for every student—and her parents—who is considering applying to boarding or private school. Even if you don't want to follow the Bush family to Andover or Facebook founder Mark Zuckerberg to Exeter, you should keep reading.

I consider our advice like training for a four-minute mile. By following our recipes for success, you will be ready to apply to any school from coast to coast. Even if you are not the next Roger Bannister, who in 1954 was the first person to run a four-minute mile, preparing at this level will only strengthen your chance of meeting any other goals. The good news, however—if you go through the process as if you are applying to the nation's elite schools, you will increase your chances of getting into every other school.

So what factors go into Top Test Prep's official rankings?

1. **Consistently sending students to the Ivy League, MIT, and Stanford.** Face it. These private and boarding schools are pricy. What is the biggest thing they provide that your neighborhood public school or run-of-the-mill private school does not? Getting students into the nation's top colleges on a regular basis.

2. **Accepting students with high standardized test scores.** We looked at the average SSAT or ISEE score of the incoming class at each school, as well as the average SAT score of their graduating classes.

3. **Having a large Alumni endowment.** Is the school well-funded? This might not seem important, but keep in mind that a school with more money in the bank has many advantages. It can pay more money for teachers and coaches, potentially attracting the best candidates for its faculty and staff. It has top-notch facilities that are beautifully maintained. And it does not feel pressure to admit more students simply to bring in more tuition revenue at the expense of lowering the overall experience.

4. **Providing low teacher-to-student ratio.** We all want smaller class sizes and more individualized instruction. So why isn't this higher on the list? Because most schools have similar average class sizes and the small differences here are not as significant.

5. **Offering a diverse student body.** A heterogeneous student body helps create a well-rounded experience for all students.

As we worked to create our rankings, the best schools on each list are comparable. The only differences are that Exeter and Andover tend to have students that score high on the SAT and accept a lower percentage of applicants. Getting into these schools is extremely competitive.

———

Top Ten Boarding Schools in America

#1 Phillips Academy Andover	Located in Andover, Massachusetts, the co-ed school is twenty-five miles north of Boston on a five-hundred-acre campus. Its most famous graduates are United States President George H. W. Bush, United States President George W. Bush, and Super Bowl winning football coach Bill Belichick. Once known for preparing its students to attend Yale, Andover now sends graduates to nearly all of the nation's elite colleges. It admits roughly one of six applicants and has an endowment of $868 million.
#2 Phillips Exeter Academy	Located in Exeter, New Hampshire, this co-ed school boasts a large student body of more than one thousand students and the largest endowment of any New England prep school, at more than $1 billion. There are 131 buildings on 671 acres. The school is noted for creating the Harkness method of teaching, where students and their teacher meet for each class at an oval table. Alumni include United States President Franklin Pierce, historian Arthur Schlesinger Jr., and Facebook founder Mark Zuckerberg.
#3 Deerfield Academy	Located in Deerfield, Massachusetts, in the western part of the state, this co-ed school is incredibly selective for its student body of roughly six hundred students. Famous alumni include King Abdullah II of Jordan, publisher Nelson Doubleday Jr., and numerous congressmen.

#4 St. Paul's School	Located on two thousand acres in Concord, New Hampshire, the co-ed school is noted for having classes six days a week as well as a diverse student body. Notable alumni include banker J. P. Morgan Jr., former FBI director Robert Mueller, Doonesbury cartoonist Garry Trudeau, and politician John Kerry.
#5 The Hotchkiss School	Located on 827 acres in Lakeville, Connecticut, in the rural northwestern part of the state, it was founded to prepare young men to attend Yale University. The co-ed school's graduates now attend nearly all of the nation's top colleges and universities. Notable alumni include *Time* magazine founders Henry Luce and Briton Hadden; automotive moguls Henry Ford II, Edsel Ford, and William Clay Ford; and Morgan Stanley founder, Harold Stanley.
#6 The Thacher School	Located in Ojai, California, eighty-five miles northwest of Los Angeles, this co-ed boarding school is located on 425 acres and is the oldest boarding school in the Golden State, founded in 1889. Nearly half of the roughly 250 students come from outside California, and the school believes strongly in outdoors education; first-year students must care for a horse and dozens of weekend camping trips are offered.
#7 Cate School	Located a short distance from the Pacific Ocean in Carpinteria along California's Central Coast, this co-ed school has roughly 250 students. New York University, the University of Southern California, the University of Chicago, and Stanford University are among the most popular college destinations for its recent graduates.

#8 Middlesex School	Located in Concord, Massachusetts, twenty miles northwest of Boston, the co-ed school has a 350-acre campus and an enrollment approaching four hundred. Notable alumni include politician Bill Richardson and actor Steve Carell.
#9 Groton School	Located in Groton, Massachusetts, in the northeast part of the state, the co-ed school has a 415-acre campus and an endowment of $330 million. With an enrollment of less than four hundred in grades eight through twelve, Groton is known for having a small community and its dedication to public service. Notable alumni include United States president Franklin Delano Roosevelt and New York Stock Exchange former president Richard Whitney.
#10 The Lawrenceville School	Located in Lawrenceville, New Jersey, the co-ed school has a seven-hundred-acre campus near Princeton and between New York City and Philadelphia. Most popular college destinations for recent graduates are Princeton University, Duke University, and Georgetown University. Notable alumni include musicians Dierks Bentley and Huey Lewis, former White House press secretary Jay Carney, and former NBC executive Brandon Tartikoff.

———

Top Ten Private Day Schools in America

#1 Trinity School	Located in New York City, this co-ed school is one of the best (if not the best) private schools in the country. Its most popular college destinations are Harvard University, Cornell University, Yale University, and Columbia University. Founded in 1709, it is the fifth-oldest school in the United States. Notable alumni include actor Humphrey Bogart, musician Yo Yo Ma, novelist Truman Capote, and tennis player John McEnroe.
#2 The Brearley School	Located in New York City, this is the best all-girls private school in the country. It has a high rate of diversity, and annually sends graduates to Yale University, Harvard University, Princeton University, and Columbia University. Notable alumni include diplomat Caroline Kennedy and actresses Kyra Sedgwick and Sigourney Weaver.
#3 Horace Mann School	All-boys school located in New York City maintains a 275-acre nature laboratory in Bethlehem, Connecticut. One of the nation's largest independent day schools, with nearly two thousand students in kindergarten through twelfth grade. Notable alumni include composer Elliott Carter, writer Jack Kerouac, and doctor and poet William Carlos Williams.
#4 The Roxbury Latin School	Founded in 1645, it is the oldest school in continuous operation in the nation. The all-boys school is located in Roxbury, Massachusetts, a neighborhood in Boston. It has a high diversity rate, and its enrollment of three hundred annually posts one of the highest average SAT scores of any school in the nation. Notable alumni include Frederick Law Olmsted Jr.

#5 Collegiate School	Founded in 1628 in New York City, it is the oldest school in the United States. The all-boys school sends a high percentage of its graduates to Ivy League schools, especially Yale University, Harvard University, Brown University, Princeton University, and the University of Pennsylvania. Notable alumni include John F. Kennedy Jr. and actor David Duchovny.
#6 Harvard-Westlake School	A co-ed school with two campuses in Los Angeles, it is known for promoting independent study. Popular college choices for graduates include Brown University, Columbia University, Cornell University, and New York University. Notable alumni include actors Maggie and Jake Gyllenhaal, Jamie Lee Curtis, Shirley Temple, and Douglas Fairbanks Jr.
#7 The Dalton School	Located in New York City, the co-ed school's graduates annually score very high on the SAT, and many of its graduates go on to Yale University, Cornell University, Brown University, and the University of Pennsylvania. Notable alumni include television anchor Anderson Cooper, actor Chevy Chase, and actress Claire Danes.
#8 Princeton Day School	Located in Princeton, New Jersey, the most popular college destinations for the co-ed school's graduates are Cornell University, the University of Pennsylvania, and Johns Hopkins University. Notable alumni include musician Mary Chapin Carpenter, journalist Marjorie Williams, and actor Christopher Reeve.

#9 National Cathedral School	The all-girls school is located in Washington, DC, and annually sends graduates to Stanford University, the University of Pennsylvania, the University of Virginia, and Princeton University. Its notable alumni include the daughters of former vice president Al Gore and producer Kara Kennedy.
#10 Sidwell Friends School	The co-ed school is located in Washington, DC, and like National Cathedral School, it educates the children of many politicians, including Albert Gore III, Chelsea Clinton, and Sasha and Malia Obama. The school does not release its average SAT score or college matriculation list.

If you're applying to one of these schools buckle up. This book will help guide you through every step of the process. And again, if you're not applying to one of these schools, the tips, pointers, and candid advice I provide will help you no matter your situation. Having counseled thousands of students at this point, I can say confidently that you should consider including at least a couple of these schools on your list. You can never go wrong aiming for the best. And consider the following schools below as we expect them to make an appearance on our top list, soon.

Top Test Prep's Rising Stars

Private School
Northfield Mt. Hermon School "NMH" (MA)
Peddie School (NJ)
Georgetown Prep School (DC)
Episcopal High School (VA)
Culver Academies (IN)

I have highlighted the above schools as those to look out for the in the future. These are schools that have made great changes in curricula and student body composition while also increasing attention and focus on nurturing the next great generation. For example, NMH now has one of the largest groups of basketball athletes attending and playing in the Ivy League with schools like Harvard and Yale.

NMH also wisely merged into one campus, thus creating a more cohesive student body. If NMH continues to be more selective in its admissions process, it could begin to stand out among schools like Exeter and Andover. Culver Academies promotes a forward-thinking concept of training students beyond the classroom, and its results are telling: more students are getting into top colleges than ever before. Georgetown Prep School ("Prep") is anchored just outside of Washington, DC, and boasts an increasingly diverse class, engaging classroom, and athletic dream team. I expect Prep to increase its standing as well in our official rankings.

I anticipate more top colleges will look to enroll students from these schools in the coming years.

And finally, one of the most important rankings of all:

*The Best College Counseling Offices in America

Every year, thousands of Top Test Prep's SAT and ACT prep clients rank their favorite college counseling offices. Guidance counseling is a martial art—managing parental expectations and balancing a massive workload while mentoring and providing candid advice to students—and these college counseling offices deserve major credit for their hard work.

We'd like to congratulate the following fifty private and public schools for being selected as having the best college counseling offices in America. Your staff and team deserve the highest recognition.

Ranking	School Name	Counselor	Public/ Private
1	The Lawrenceville School	Holly Burks Becker	Private
2	Phillips Exeter Academy	Betsy Dolan	Private
3	Trinity School	Lawrence J. Momo	Private
4	Crystal Springs Uplands School	Jennifer Carleton	Private
5	Brearley School	Carolyn W. Clark	Private
6	Thomas Jefferson High School for Science and Technology	Eileen Kropf	Public
7	Northfield Mount Hermon	Peter Jenkins	Private

8	Georgetown Preparatory High School	Patrick Gallagher	Private
9	Oxford Academy	Janet Low	Public
10	The Thacher School	Maria Morales-Kent	Private
11	California Academy Of Mathematics And Science	Barry T. Baker	Public
12	Walt Whitman High School	Jennifer Higgins	Public
13	St. Paul's School	Timothy W. Pratt	Private
14	Lakeside School	Ari Worthman	Private
15	Cate School	Anne Love Hall	Private
16	Middlesex School	Matthew J. DeGreeff	Private
17	Horace Mann School	Canh Oxelson	Private
18	Deerfield Academy	Mark Spencer	Private
19	The Spence School	Dana Boocock Crowell	Private
20	Groton School	Megan Harlan	Private
21	The Roxbury-Latin School	Thomas E. Walsh, Jr.	Private
22	Milton Academy	Rod Skinner	Private
23	Concord Academy	Kate Peltz	Private
24	Pine View School	Lance Bergman	Public
25	Winston Churchill High School	Robin Moore	Public
26	The Hotchkiss School	Richard Hazelton	Private
27	Loomis Chaffee School	Webb Trenchard	Private
28	The Dalton School	Robert S. Koppert	Private
29	The Winsor School	David Clarke	Private
30	College Preparatory School	Martin Bonilla	Private
31	University High School	Treya Allen	Public
32	Wootton High School	Lynda Hitchcock	Public
33	Walter Payton College Preparatory High School	Lance Paulsen	Public
34	Georgetown Day School	Barbara Bergman	Private
35	Gwinnett School of Mathematics, Science and Technology	Meg Scheid	Public
36	St. Albans School for Boys	Nikki Magaziner Mills	Private
37	San Francisco University High School	Jonathan Reider	Private

38	Latin School of Chicago	Elizabeth Pleshette	Private
39	Richard Montgomery High School	John Randall	Public
40	Sidwell Friends School	Lauren Carter	Private
41	Stanton College Preparatory School	Bob Turba	Public
42	Georgetown Visitation	Tara Maglio	Private
43	The Hockaday School	Carol Wasden	Private
44	St. John's College High School	Elizabeth Lightfoot	Private
45	Maret School	Blake Spraggins	Private
46	Chapin School	Karey Boals	Private
47	Princeton Day School	Sarah Graham	Private
48	National Cathedral School	Erin Johnston	Private
49	Rye Country Day School	Rosita Fernandez-Rojo	Private
50	The Potomac School	Mike Oligmueller	Private

Let us know if you want to include your school in these rankings, or believe they belong in this select group of schools:

Call (800) 501-7737, or visit us at http://toptestprep.com/learn-more

Congratulations again to these selected well-deserved schools.

CHAPTER 4

FIND YOUR X-FACTOR

*"You are so busy being YOU that you have no idea
how utterly unprecedented you are."*
John Green, *The Fault in Our Stars*

I have counseled thousands of teenagers and their families on the private and boarding school application process. And yet I can say with certainty that every student brings a set of circumstances that makes her stand apart. For instance, I will never forget Julie, who came to Top Test Prep a few years ago seeking advice on how to navigate the waitlists at several schools.

Julie lived in California. She was meticulous and organized, and she had everything lined up well in advance as she navigated the admissions process. She had researched the schools, taking long looks at their websites. She had taken the SSAT in the fall and scored well. She submitted her applications on time.

As she brought me up to speed on her process, I reviewed the applications she had submitted. Immediately, I noticed a few red flags, particularly in her essay and personal statements, that I was sure had held her back.

First, Julie had not visited all of the schools to which she applied. This might seem normal, as Julie was applying to schools both close to home in California and three thousand miles away. While it is a challenge for West Coast residents to travel to the elite prep schools in the Northeast, not visiting those campuses creates a bigger problem, as the applicant remains at arm's length from getting to know the schools. If the student doesn't visit, the campus remains one-dimensional, existing only in what you can see on brochures, virtual tours, and websites. Visiting a campus brings a school to life and allows prospective students the opportunity to get to know the school—much like the admissions officers need to get to know you. All of the items put out by the schools are meant to show the school in the best possible light. Those beautiful dogwood trees in the school brochures are not in bloom year-round! Remember, there is no replacement for the campus visit! The campus visit is especially important when an applicant writes her essays, as it is preferable for the applicant to demonstrate her interest in the school and note how she will fit in on campus.

Second, despite not having a personal feel for several schools, Julie tried to tailor her personal statements to each school where she applied, a move that I would advise against even if she had visited each school. The essays included in her applications for schools in California, with which she was more familiar and comfortable, had an easy, free-flowing feel. But the writing in her applications to East Coast schools had a stodgy, herky-jerky feel with little cohesion.

My initial instinct was that Julie's writing needed to demonstrate who she is, keeping in mind that the Hawk, the Scout, and the Veteran would be reading these pieces to get to know her. Instead of writing multiple personal statements, Julie should have written the best possible statement and made sure the writing was in her voice—not what she thought the admissions officers would want to read. She had a 3.95 unweighted grade point average and an SSAT over 2100. Her application was not going to be rejected because of her scores, and it was apparent that she cared about the process and planned well. But Julie needed to do a better job ensuring her writing allowed the Hawk, the Veteran, and the Scout the chance to get to know her.

This is the elusive X-factor—making certain that your passion comes across on paper.

Remember, in the previous chapter, we defined passion as the person, place, subject, event, or thing that inspires you and moves you to take a leadership role in some area of your life. Well, now we have to make sure your passion comes alive so admissions officers feel it. I cannot stress this enough!

Going back to Julie, her passion was soccer. She was a strong player, certainly someone who was going to play for her high school team and potentially in college. She had been playing since she was a youngster and soon joined a travel team. She attended soccer clinics and went to an overnight soccer camp in the summer. Her travel team was noted for producing several top players who went on to excel at every step against top competition. As a soccer player, Julie had a strong identity.

But because she had not visited the Northeast schools, she was not comfortable expressing her passion for soccer to those schools. She was worried about how it would be perceived if it was a sport that was her passion. She did not realize that the athletic programs at these schools were strong or that the admissions officers were involved in athletics. While her application to the Thacher School was an easy read and Julie's passion oozed off the page, her applications to East Coast schools lacked such enthusiasm. Just because a school has an elite academic reputation, do not assume the school focuses only on academics and not on athletics or any other extracurricular activity. If you are passionate about sports, Exeter, Andover, NMH, and others are not so uptight. Julie automatically thought, "Oh, it's Andover. Their students must study all day. If my personal statement is focused on sports, I won't fit in there." Her writing reflected this. Her passion for soccer needed to be displayed better. **Remember, the personal statement must be about you and demonstrate who you are as a person, so make it personal!**

We worked with Julie to help her get off the waitlist and into her first choice. She contacted the soccer coach, writing what amounted to another personal statement, detailing her passion for school and her interest in playing for the school. Despite the flaws in her application, she was such a strong candidate that we were able to help her get into Lawrenceville. However, if you were Julie, wouldn't you have wanted to have as many options as possible?

Myth: Your X-factor has to be academics. After all, we are talking about applying to the nation's elite schools. These schools want only the best students, so you need to show your interest in school work.

Fact: Your X-factor can be anything, from schoolwork to sports to video games. Don't worry about what you think schools want to hear. Make sure to demonstrate your passion.

That brings me to the Top Test Prep top-ten lists of the nation's top boarding schools and the top private day schools. These schools excel at helping their students mature academically and socially. Their counselors provide strong guidance throughout the college application process. These schools are known for sending nearly all of their students to elite colleges and universities. Whether it is innately developed by the students themselves or a result of conversations the students have had with their parents, students at these elite private and boarding schools are driven from day one and always look to take advantage of opportunities. In short the students at these schools are **passionate!**

Think about it. If you are going to spend up to $45,000 a year—potentially a quarter of a million dollars or more before college—there must be a value added. Unless you are Warren Buffett, that is a lot of money. The value here, for most students and their families, is matriculating to a top college or university and positioning the student to succeed in life.

That is a big measure of why parents will invest so much money on high school.

I am a firm believer that 80 percent of your success can be attributed to your environment and those with whom you are surrounded. Only 20 percent is genetic. So if excellence surrounds every corner of the campus, it impacts a school's students. If you visit Andover, you quickly notice the atmosphere of high expectations and self-motivation. There are students who excel in sports, but they don't mind being the smartest person in the class either. In public schools and even some private schools, you do not feel comfortable being both. At Andover and other schools on our top-ten lists, being smart in class and a star athlete is welcomed, if not encouraged. This is important for student-athletes, like Julie, to remember. By surrounding yourself with motivated, driven peers, you will be pushed to perform at a high level.

Parent tip: I never cease to be amazed at how geographically segmented this space is, particularly among boarding schools. Many people in different parts of the country are oblivious to some of these top schools. Maybe they have heard of Andover because of the Bush family, but the name recognition of many of these schools is lacking if you do not live nearby. It is important to take the time to review all of the schools on our lists and consider their strengths. Even if a school is far away or lacks the high profile that some other schools tote, it might offer the best environment for your child to succeed. Always have a criteria for what you are looking for in a school.

*** The Numbers Game ***

Remember, most of the applicants to top schools have high SSAT or ISEE scores and grade point averages. Can an admissions officer discern between a B at a public school in Texas and a B at a private school in California? Of course not. It is hard enough to do this at the high school level where some schools are better known, but very few middle schools carry a reputation that makes this possible. What the Hawk, the Scout, and the Veteran look for are consistency and pattern. Does a student repeatedly get top grades with no dips throughout the school year? Is the student seeking out advanced and honors courses when they are available? If you attend a public school with a mediocre academic reputation but seek out every opportunity you can to challenge yourself, that's a good sign. Loading up on honors courses shows a student who strives to improve. Conversely, if you attend a private middle school noted for its academic brand but fail to demonstrate how you have challenged yourself in the classroom, that too will be noticed by the admissions officers.

Additionally, I believe there are three components to the admissions process: objective, purgatory, and subjective.

The **objective** portion of the application is a student's score on the SSAT or ISEE. Regardless of any special considerations permitted to complete these tests, the questions are the same for every student. Each test is scored the same, making it easy to compare scores for different students. There is little interpretation when it comes to analyzing these results, you either have a good score or you do not. In my chart this column is on the left, and when a student has a sufficiently high score, I visualize a green arrow pointing right to the next step in the process.

The **purgatory**, a student's grade point average and their transcript, is a bit more complicated. It is in the middle of the chart and is more difficult to assess. Just because a student has a high GPA, does that mean they are intelligent and motivated? If the student has a 3.1 GPA, should that count against the student? Or does their school have a grading system where As are difficult to obtain? The land of purgatory is tough to judge and won't be a deal maker or deal breaker, but being able to place another green arrow in this column is helpful.

The **subjective** component is a student's essays, personal statement, interviews, brag sheet, recommendations, extracurricular activities, and any other special interests or talents. It is subjective because it is incumbent on the Hawk, the Scout, and the Veteran to judge each applicant individually and assess whether the she will be a good match. It is in this subjective component that the applicant must be able to share her passion!

Myth: Focus most of your time on the parts of your application that are weakest.

Fact: Even if one part of your application needs more work than others, you still need to spend an appropriate amount of time on each facet.

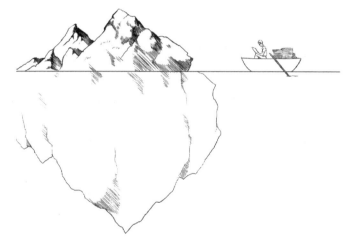

- ◆ The tip of the Iceberg is for students with great test scores and grades.

- ◆ The line where the tip meets the bottom of the iceberg is for students with good but not great test scores and grades.

- ◆ The bottom of the iceberg is for students with test scores and grades that need help.

Now let's look at three types of applicants and where they should focus their efforts in the application process:

- ◆ **Your test scores and grades are excellent: SSAT or ISEE in the 90th percentile or higher and GPA 3.85 and above.**
  You should spend 80 percent of your time in the application process working on essays and the personal statement and 20 percent on test preparation and trying to improve your grades. Most of the students applying to the schools on our top-ten lists fall into this category.

Your job is not to present any red flags. You are going to ace the objective column. And you will have no problem in the land of purgatory; though it is difficult to compare the transcripts of different students, your grades are splendid. The subjective part, however, is where you need to try to set yourself apart. While you pass muster with your test score and grades, you need to find a way to stand out from your peers. Know that the top schools, such as Andover, Exeter, and Deerfield, have a deluge of applicants with excellent test scores and grades, so you must prove to the admissions committee why your application is better than the rest. Focus on the essays. Make sure your recommendations are authentic, reflect who you are, and allow the Hawk, the Scout, and the Veteran to get to know you. **You must demonstrate your passion!** Passion is something you cannot make up and cannot fake.

Look at Julie's example. Objectively, she should have been accepted. She had the test score and grades. She was organized and prepared. But her writing did not let the admissions staff understand who she is as a person, and it cost her. If Julie had spent more time on her personal statement and essays, I am certain she would have been admitted everywhere she applied. She had the correct mind-set approaching the application process. But she forgot what I told you at the beginning of this book: admissions officers are people. People are excited to know students who have something to offer besides their grades.

The sad thing is there are plenty of students who assume that having the grades and test scores is sufficient for them to be accepted. It just doesn't happen that way! If it did, why would schools make you fill out the rest of an application they had no intention of reading? Just send in your scores and be admitted, right? Of course not. If you don't show passion on paper in your application and in person during your campus visit and interview, you end up looking like a robotic cyborg.

♦ **Your test scores and grades are good but not great and fit into the median range of applicants: SSAT or ISEE in the 75th to 90th percentile and GPA 3.4 to 3.85.**
You should put 60 percent of your focus on test preparation and improving your SSAT or ISEE scores and 40 percent on your essays and grade point averages.

Remember James, the student who came to me at the last minute a few years back? He did not even contact us until January 12, and, even then, it was only at the urging of his parents! Despite being from Boston and so close to elite schools, such as Roxbury Latin, Noble and Greenough, and Milton Academy, and with classmates who also were applying to these very schools, James was naïve about what needed to be done. He did not research schools and did not know how to prepare for the SSAT. The third of four brothers with divorced parents, his grades were so-so, and a quick look at his transcript showed a student who was not motivated.

First, we encouraged James and his family to visit some schools and tour campuses of the schools in which they were interested. This did the trick. By seeing the campuses for himself and meeting the students who attended these schools, James was compelled to take control of his situation, and he became willing to work hard to accomplish his goals! It was the campus visits that opened his eyes to the possibilities and instilled an inner drive in James.

Then we started to work with James on the SSAT. The first time he took the test, his scores were adequate at best, in the 600s on each of the three sections. But with our help, James raised his score by more than 200 points to the 2200s! Maybe this new drive would convince James to dedicate himself in the classroom—which would be great, of course—but for our purposes, there was not much point in trying to get James to raise his grade point average. Even if he somehow managed to get straight As, it was the second semester of eighth grade, and his new grades would be posted when his applications were already submitted.

Where James excelled the most—and why I believe he was able to gain admission to three schools—was in **making sure schools understood his passion**. James did a great job here! James had boundless energy for music. He loved to use music technology to compose new pieces, and he was a standout guitar player. I vividly remember that James composed a series of guitar solos, and we decided to send it directly to the music department at each school where he was applying. I have seen this done rarely, where a student reached out to another member of the school community, and I know that made James shine because the head of each music department contacted the admissions office to let them know about James! To the Hawk, the Scout, and the Veteran, this gave James the appearance that he was enthusiastic and engaging.

James was limited by his late start in the process and the fact that many schools already had their incoming students selected, but he was able to gain admission to the schools that still had spots remaining: Andover, Groton, and Tabor—three pretty darn good schools!

- **Your test scores and grades need some work: SSAT or ISEE under 600 per section and GPA under 3.4.**
  So your numbers are going to attract the attention of admissions officers who tend to only disqualify applicants based on their test scores and GPAs. That is not the best thing, obviously, but we can work with it.

The way I look at the application process, admissions officers use the objective component of the SSAT or ISEE scores to know how they should view the purgatory component of your grade point average. If they get a green light in both of these areas, then they move onto the subjective component, your essays, personal statement, and recommendations.

But students in this area will not be able to improve their GPAs overnight. Their best bet is to go all out and spend 80 percent of their time on test preparation with the hope of raising their SSAT or ISEE scores to a level that suggests they are capable of doing high-level work. The other 20 percent of their efforts should be on the subjective components, getting all of their essays and recommendations in perfect shape and making sure their passion comes across. But remember, these students still need to be authentic in their applications. If you have mediocre grades and test scores, it will not seem genuine if your essays read like published short stories and your recommendations make it seem like you are the valedictorian of your class. The tip I have for you is to write about an exceptional life experience you have had or your unique background.

If you don't have the best grades, maybe the top schools aren't for you—and that is fine. But if you have your heart set on a certain school, by all means please apply. Every boarding school and private school opens itself up to some applicants who would not seem to fit their ideal candidate profile. I guarantee it. If the schools did not do this, there would be empty slots in each matriculating class, and the student body would be homogeneous. Does that mean this underachieving student is certain to get in to the school of their choice? Of course not. So don't be disappointed when the rejection letter comes in the mail. But that should not keep you from applying in the first place.

Application tip: This goes for all students, as nobody is perfect. In the short amount of real estate in each application, there is no time for excuses. The Scout, the Hawk, or the Veteran only have so much time for each application. Don't let them spend any time they are focused on your application reading about your shortcomings.

Think about it this way. When buying a car, does a salesperson point out a dent or the fact that the car you have your eyes on is a total gas guzzler? Heck no! Surely the salesperson knows about any imperfections or areas in which the product he is selling does not measure up, but instead of telling you about these, the salesperson is focused on the positives and trying to get you to picture yourself in this car. If you point out a flaw, a good salesperson is prepared with the proper answer. "That dent is so minor and this is such a perfect color that only when the light hits it at this particular angle will anyone notice." If there are some gaps in your application, let the admissions officers identify these and ask you about them. Let them decide if these gaps pose a significant problem or if the gaps are a minor hurdle to overcome. No one is perfect. Don't be afraid to apply. What's the worst that can happen? They will say no? Don't regret it later and think about what you could have done differently.

*** Other Frequently Asked Questions ***

Is affirmative action significant in the private and boarding school application process?

Absolutely, though I do not think it is as much of a consideration as it is for the college admittance process, where *U.S. News & World Report* releases its annual rankings. A homogeneous private school is not good. Affirmative action can help. If you want affirmative action to work in your favor, you have to talk about how your circumstances have impacted it, which can be tough to do. But if you can talk about it in a coherent way, private schools know their goal is to provide students the opportunity to attend top colleges, and enrolling minorities can help promote the boarding and private schools. It is a self-perpetuating cycle.

Do legacies have a significant advantage?

Yes, if the alum has been involved to some extent. If the alum has little interaction with the school and is not active in the school community, it will not help much. But if the alum has donated to the school or helped with interviews in the application process, being a legacy will be beneficial. Keep in mind, though, that the application process is much more competitive than it used to be. Just being a legacy no longer guarantees you a spot in the school of your choice. The old-boy network has diversified, especially after Andover received its share of attention while alumnus George W. Bush served as our nation's forty-third president. The world of boarding schools has opened up, and it is not as insulated as it once was.

Will applying early help my chance of being admitted?

Yes. This is one more edge for an applicant to use to their advantage. Schools desire students who want to matriculate. The sooner your application is received, the better chance you will be accepted. This is crucial.

Do recommendations matter?

Yes. But remember, I have read thousands of recommendations and have yet to read my first bad recommendation. Typically, they are self-serving. The way to stand out is to use them in a way that shows your passion!

Should I explain my weaknesses in an application?

No. The application is there to help you, not to hinder your chances of admission. Don't give the admissions office any ammunition to reject your application.

CHAPTER 5

HOW YOU CAN PREPARE FOR THE SSAT OR ISEE

The thought of sitting at a desk for two to three hours and taking a test that could determine the course of your life is frightening for anyone, even an adult. Now imagine you are a twelve-year-old sixth grader or even a fourteen-year-old eighth grader, with your No. 2 pencils sharpened, walking through the door for this critical exam. Scary stuff, right?

As someone who has counseled thousands of students and their families, I am here to reassure and guide you through taking the Secondary School Admission Test (SSAT) or the Independent School Entrance Exam (ISEE). These tests are essential to your chances of gaining admission to the private or boarding school of your choice. But remember what we learned in Chapter 1: admissions officers are people, too. They are professionals and know they are dealing with youngsters taking an important test like this for the first time.

Trust me. Schools are aware that their applicants are not yet fully developed as students. Admissions officers are charged with the task of projecting what an applicant will be like in two or three years if the student matriculates to their school. Even the nine months between the time a student files an application and when the student matriculates at her new school can make a significant difference.

I grew up in a school district that, for better or worse, did not emphasize testing. I had no idea how to prepare for the SSAT. My academic prowess did not mature until I was fifteen or sixteen years old, though my father will say that I am not mature yet!

I would like to teach you what I learned from my own journey to prep school as well as my dealings with countless students in the same situation you find yourself to take you through this process. Follow my advice, and you will be prepared when you walk into the classroom to take the SSAT or ISEE.

> **Parent tip:** No matter how well your child has performed in the classroom or how calm and poised they might appear, they will be nervous for this test. It is a big moment and the first time your child has done anything like this. Do your best to be reassuring and help your child prepare. Your goal should be to persuade your child to start early and treat this test preparation as if it is a part-time job. It takes plenty of time and effort to be fully prepared, but this will be well worth it.

One student I will never forget is Steven, who came to Top Test Prep several years ago because his family wanted him to attend boarding school. Steven had excellent grades and had taken responsibility for the application process. He was well organized, had obtained the applications he wanted, and went on campus visits in the fall. It was as if Steven heard my advice even before he came through our doors. Additionally, his profile was well rounded with extracurricular interests, and he had scored well in school on state-mandated standardized testing. His English teacher had written a terrific recommendation that focused on Steven's inner drive and desire to challenge himself. In short, Steven was a terrific candidate for admission. If he could add a high score on the SSAT, he would be a no-brainer for the Hawk, the Scout, and the Veteran!

But like every other student, Steven doubted himself when it came to taking the SSAT. When he sat down for his first practice test, his initial reaction was paralyzed fear. And this is someone who had his act together, so you can imagine what other students might be like!

When taking these practice tests, students should simulate exact test conditions. If you are taking the SSAT at nine o'clock on a Saturday morning, then you should take all of your practice tests at nine o'clock on Saturday mornings. Don't take the practice test at the kitchen table or on a family-room sofa. Find a desk—just as it will be when you take the test in a classroom. Both the SSAT and

ISEE provide the exact timeline for taking their tests, including breaks—you should follow this schedule when taking practice tests. Just like running a race, it helps to know the course.

The only exception should be if you want to allow a few minutes less time per section so that when you take the actual test it will seem easier. Keeping with our running analogy, this would be like putting on ankle weights while trying to build your endurance during training runs. On race day, when you take off the weights, everything becomes much easier.

I cannot overstate the importance of taking these practice tests as if they are the actual exams! Take them in a quiet room without distractions. Just like when visiting an admissions office, leave your cell phone behind. Don't be tempted by Facebook, e-mail or social media. Have an adult time each section as if you are taking the actual exam.

Test-taking tip: When taking practice tests, do not just guess at answers. Be able to explain how you arrived at your answer. If you are unable to do this for a specific problem, circle it and go over it later with an adult who can help you understand the problem. This will help in the long run as you become an independent thinker.

Getting back to Steven, he scored 2010 on his first SSAT practice test, which is good but not great and certainly not in line with the rest of his body of work. He had room to improve, and we set a schedule for him to take a practice test each week. We set a goal of trying to correctly answer one more problem each week than the previous exam. Sounds easy enough, right? Because Steven started his test prep early, we had time to work together and prepare as we introduced several Top Test Top test-taking strategies. Steven steadily improved his practice scores, and when he took the real SSAT, he posted a score over 2300. He got into every school where he applied. Steven went from feeling paralyzed to being empowered, which is awesome! He ended up going to Lawrenceville.

Parent tip: When helping your child prepare, start with what they already know and merge in what they need to learn. Build their confidence. Their scores are not going to shoot up three hundred points in one week. Preparing for the SSAT and ISEE is a gradual process. It is like training for a marathon, where a runner builds stamina over time. Your child needs at least thirty days of continual preparation and needs to treat test preparation as if it is a part-time job. I recommend trying to commit two hours a day for three months! If you are reading this book and do not have thirty days to prepare, do not expect to maximize your child to reach their potential.

While the SSAT and ISEE are essential components of the private and boarding school admissions process, the Hawk, the Scout, and the Veteran do not scrutinize your SSAT or ISEE score as much as college admissions officers judge applicants' SAT or ACT scores. Private and boarding school admissions officers understand a twelve- or thirteen-year-old is going to be different when she is fifteen or sixteen. Just look at me. I was a different person after just one year at NMH than I was at Pleasant Grove Middle School in Texarkana.

With this in mind, let's look at some frequently asked questions about the SSAT and ISEE.

What are the different levels of the SSAT and ISEE?

The SSAT is administered on three levels: Elementary for students currently in grades three through four, Middle for grades five through seven, and Upper for grades eight through eleven.

The Elementary Level SSAT is comprised of three multiple-choice sections, and a writing sample and takes one hour fifty minutes. The Middle Level SSAT and Upper Level SSAT are divided into five sections: two math, one verbal, one reading comprehension, and an unscored essay that is sent to schools to which you apply. There also is an unscored experimental section for administrators to work on development of new tests. The Middle Level SSAT and Upper Level SSAT take two hours fifty minutes, not including breaks.

The ISEE has four levels: Primary for students currently in grades one through three, Lower for grades four through five, Middle for grades six through seven, and Upper for grades eight through eleven. The Primary Level ISEE takes one hour and includes sections on reading and math and a short writing sample. The other ISEE exams have five portions: verbal reasoning, quantitative reasoning, reading comprehension, math, and an unscored essay. The Lower Level ISEE takes two hours twenty minutes; the Middle Level ISEE and Upper Level ISEE take two hours forty minutes, not including breaks.

Note to readers: These schedules are subject to change annually. Check TopTestPrep.com to confirm.

Can you take the SSAT and ISEE multiple times, and how will the admissions committee view this?

You can take the SSAT an unlimited number of times. The ISEE may be taken only once in each application cycle.

Having said this, I urge you not to take the SSAT more than twice, and even then, you should retake the test only if you are certain to improve your score. You need to show an upward trend if you retake the test. The admissions committee will view taking the test too many times negatively.

Of course, you should take the SSAT or the ISEE in the fall and only after you have done thorough test prep. By taking the SSAT in the fall, you allow time to get your score and potentially have time to go back and study again if you want to retake the test.

> **Test-taking tip:** Prepare as if you will take the SSAT only once. If you enter the test planning to take it again, you will not be in the right mind-set to perform your best. Also, if you take the test and are not sure whether you can score better, do not take it again. My rule of thumb is to take the test no more than twice. The more you take it, the worse it looks.

Myth: There is no need to worry about doing well on the SSAT. An applicant can take this test as many times as necessary to achieve a high score.

Fact: While the SSAT allows students to take the test as many times as they desire, you should treat each test as if it is the only time you will take it. If you do feel a need to retake the SSAT, do not take the test more than twice. If you take the test more than twice, it will raise a red flag on your application.

Should you take the SSAT or the ISEE?

The tests are similar, except for a few small items. The SSAT has analogies, and the ISEE does not. When it comes to scoring, the SSAT penalizes students for wrong answers and the ISEE does not. Keep this in mind if you are merely guessing, as being reckless can cost you on the SSAT.

The SSAT is more widely known nationally and internationally, and it is offered more widely. The ISEE should be your preferred test if you are looking at the top private day schools in New England, such as Horace Mann or Greenwich Country Day.

If it does not matter to the schools you are applying to, I recommend the SSAT because of its reliability as a predictor for success on the SAT. Also, if necessary, the SSAT allows you the ability to retake the test if you score poorly.

Myth: The SSAT is easier than the ISEE, or vice versa.

Fact: Neither test is harder than the other. Some students do better on the SSAT; others do better on the ISEE. Just focus on one—usually, SSAT for boarding school applicants—and do a good job the first time you take the test.

What scores do you need to be competitive for top schools?

As we discussed in Chapter 3, there is no minimum score needed to get into any school, nor is there a score that guarantees admission. In general if you are applying to the schools on the Top Test Prep top-ten lists, you should have a score in the 90th percentile or above. Admissions officers will err on the side of caution, however, because there is a trend of students devoting themselves to test prep and improving their SSAT scores after their campus visits and interviews. Remember that these visits often provide inspiration and motivation for students after they return home and many become committed to improving their SSAT scores.

A school's median score is 2200 but you have a 2010. Should you even bother applying?

Absolutely. As we discussed in Chapter 3, even if your profile does not match up with the typical student admitted by a school, the worst that can happen is you will not be accepted. So what?

Admissions officers understand that you are going to mature throughout your schooling and try to include this in their decision-making process. Admissions officers know this and leave some wiggle room for applicants on their SSAT and ISEE scores. So if you are interested in a school, but your scores fall short of the school's median numbers, you should still apply.

Myth: If you do not meet the median SSAT and grade point average for a specific school, you should not waste your time applying there.

Fact: Forge full-steam ahead with the application for any school that interests you. The median numbers are just that; some students will be admitted with scores lower than the median. Just don't be disappointed if you do not gain admission to these schools.

How does a good SSAT or ISEE score help my application? How does a bad SSAT or ISEE score hurt my application?

Good test scores will neither guarantee your admission, nor will poor test scores automatically disqualify your application. As we have discussed, good test scores keep your application rolling toward admission, while poor test scores require you to wow the admissions committee in some other way. It is important to find your X-factor and make an impression on the admissions committee regardless of your test scores.

*** How to Study for Your SSAT and ISEE ***

Neither the SSAT nor the ISEE make their tests available publicly. The ISEE posts sample questions online. The SSAT provides a limited number of practice problems, and you can purchase practice tests online. It is important to attempt to answer as many questions from the test makers as possible. At Top Test Prep, we use primary sources all the time, testing our students with the SSAT practice tests and all the ISEE sample questions we have collected over the years. Additionally, there are several books containing practice tests for both of these exams. I recommend purchasing these and taking these practice exams while simulating testing conditions, as we have discussed. Also, if you have the ability to take a prep class or work with a private tutor, I recommend doing this. Having a teacher, coach, or mentor will provide a level of comfort with the test. This person will motivate you. A good tutor is somebody who tells you what you need to hear, not what you want to hear.

I remember one student, Robin, who came to Top Test Prep a few years ago having never seen a big test. Her parents had attended Andover and Exeter, so Robin felt pressure to follow in their footsteps. However, she had skated through elementary school—in a strong public school system in suburban Washington—without being challenged in the classroom. When we first went over the SSAT with her, she was intimidated. But as we shared our test-taking strategies and helped Robin become comfortable with the SSAT, her scores shot up, going from the low 30th percentiles on her initial practice tests to the 90th percentile on her real SSAT! This does not happen all the time, but it is not uncommon either. Many students—even those like Robin whose parents are familiar with the private and boarding school admissions—do not realize what they are getting into and need assistance navigating their way. You will be amazed how much improvement can be made if you approach SSAT or ISEE preparation in the proper way. With her improved score and thorough resume, Robin went to Deerfield.

Here are some of the studying tips that we use at Top Test Prep.

Regardless of which section you are working on, read the problem out loud.
Read it slowly and carefully. Too often, students rush through things, trying to finish as quickly as possible instead of focusing on how they get to the finish line. Many other test prep companies recommend reading the questions first then going back and skimming through the content, trying to notice pertinent information, and picking out the answers. By reading out loud, you will focus on what you are reading. Make sure that you understand what you are reading—this is incredibly important. Don't just scan or gloss over the words. Try to digest everything you read and what it means. Read things twice if necessary. The people who compose SSAT and ISEE questions often throw in extraneous details in an attempt to confuse students—don't let this happen to you!

When studying math, we advocate two key concepts: build confidence and "unwrap" the problem. For starters you should learn how to solve the hardest problems first and then work back to easier problems. By learning the fundamentals of solving difficult problems, you create a foundation to solve less complex problems. And guess what? Most of the problems on the SSAT and ISEE will not fall into the "most difficult" category.

Unwrapping the problem is an acronym for Top Test Prep's four-step strategy that goes along with reading a question and understanding what you read.

1. **Un**derline the prompt—what is being asked?

2. **Wr**ite the relevant formulas and equation next to the problem.

3. **A**ssemble the equation.

4. **Pl**ug in the numbers and solve…and don't forget to double-check your answer!

When working on reading comprehension, the most important skill for a student to learn is how to become an active reader.
Most of the time, when we read—whether it is a book, *The Economist, The Wall Street Journal, Deadspin,* or whatever—there is a tendency to gloss over words and not inspect and comprehend the meaning of each and every word. Schoolteachers expect their students to read a book and afterward write a report on what they have read.

Top Test Prep's goal is for you to be active and take notes, usually written and in the margins, while you read. These notes should be only a few words and refer to the author's point of view and tone. Doing this keeps you involved while reading. Think of it as the difference between hearing and listening. While daydreaming in class, you might hear a teacher talking, but you do not listen to what the teacher says. If you are actively taking notes, you will listen to the teacher!

Also, after reading a passage, we encourage students to go back and write a clever four- or five-word title for this passage. This also is geared toward making you an active reader. If you understand what you have read and are able to title a passage, it puts you in position of being the author. We all know that the author is the best person to explain what she has written.

In writing, there are three tenets on which students should focus: organization, strong evidence, and natural transitions.

Whether you are writing an essay or personal statement as part of your application or writing an essay as part of the SSAT or ISEE, you should follow these principles. Your writing should begin with a strong introductory thesis. Follow this by presenting "evidence" or facts that support your point of view. If time and space permit, provide counterexamples. Do not worry what admissions officers will think of your topic and the argument you make when they read your writing. They are not scoring your ideas! Remember Julie from Chapter 3, who worried about what the admissions committee would think if she showed her passion for soccer when she should have concentrated on showing her passion for anything? Well, in this instance, instead of showing your passion, you are showing your ability to write and present a coherent argument. You will see whether your writing has natural transitions and a clean flow when you read it aloud. If you read it aloud and there are instances where it seems halting or awkward, this is a cue to go back and rewrite.

Vocabulary is important on the SSAT and ISEE. We have a three-prong method for learning vocabulary.

1. **Memorize** the word.

2. **Use it** in a sentence.

3. **Distinguish it** from similar words.

The last item is the most difficult. Consider this example: lackadaisical and indolent are two words that mean lazy. Be able to distinguish between these words and know when to use each. Here, someone who is lackadaisical puts forth a half-hearted effort, whereas someone who is indolent just wants to avoid working hard or physical or mental exertion. You should learn fifteen to twenty new words weekly. Add in new synonyms and antonyms that you will learn during the course of preparation, and this will lead you to learn hundreds of new words in a short amount of time.

Again, instead of just memorizing new words or facts, I cannot stress enough the importance of doing actual learning while preparing for the SSAT and ISEE. Instead of just figuring out the answer, students need to learn to explain how they arrived at the answer. If they can do this, they will be able to handle just about every question that comes their way.

The Candlestick Effect

As you prepare for the SSAT or ISEE, I want to share with you one of my most important test-taking tips. This is so simple that it might sound silly, but I promise it works. I call it the "candlestick effect," and it will both light and spark your memory.

Throughout the last ten years at Top Test Prep, I have used this interesting way to remember things. When you are studying for the exam—hopefully, not just the week before, but at least thirty days in advance—you want to use as many senses as possible. You sit down and use your sense of smell, sense of taste, sense of hearing, and sense of touch—all the senses we have as human beings! As a mnemonic device, when you are studying, have a candle in the room that emits a scent. Play some light classical music in the background—not overbearing music but something that, for example, might help you remember that moment when you realized the key to a problem was reading the whole thing through first. Eat a light snack, though you do not want to overdo it and get tired. Combine the sense of touch—use a pen or number-two pencils and paper. Touching, as opposed to using a computer and just clicking with a mouse, can make you remember better.

The point here is that you want to combine as many senses as possible so when you get into the actual test, these little items will pop into your head. It works like a charm! No other test prep companies have recognized this mnemonic tool, but it does wonders for our students, particularly on the SSAT and ISEE. Parents, you need to do this and help set the mood for your children when they study so they feel comfortable and use as many senses as possible. These memories will trigger flashbacks when your children take the tests for real.

I have had many students come back to me after the SSAT or ISEE and remark how they remembered ways to solve problems during the exams. It is the same way my dad studied for medical school, and it does work. When you are studying for something, use as many senses as possible.

———

As we developed our strategies at Top Test Prep, I wanted our advice to be different and innovative. While we have composed a plan that will bolster your SSAT and ISEE scores, repeatedly we return to the same premise: students need to prepare properly, think for themselves, and be able to explain how they arrived at an answer.

This one idea permeates nearly everything we have discussed so far, from beginning the application process and taking ownership of it to choosing personal statement topics and, now, to preparing for the biggest test a student has taken in her young life.

If you are organized and have a timely plan of attack, you will be able to tackle the application process, including the SSAT or ISEE. While these tests at first might scare you, if you follow my advice, you will conquer them.

CHAPTER 6

HELPFUL ARTICLES WRITTEN BY TOP TEST PREP'S TUTORS

How to Prep for the SSAT: Five Great Tips to Get Ready

You are starting to prepare for the SSAT, but where do you begin? You have most likely never taken a standardized test of this length and depth. Take a deep breath, and follow these five tips.

1. **Start practicing earlier and often.** The earlier you start your SSAT prep, the better off you will be. In this situation starting early means beginning test prep at least three months before the test date. Cramming for a test is never a good idea, much less for a three-hour one. Studying months before the test will not only allow you to absorb the material but also learn proper test-taking strategies. This brings me to my next point.

2. **Do real practice tests!** Even if you are confident with the material, you will want to ensure that you can solve all the questions in a timely manner. Taking full-length practice tests will measure your mental endurance as well as your ability to finish all the sections. Having all the knowledge in the world won't help if you suffer from test anxiety or do not properly gauge your time.

3. **Study your vocabulary.** While the SSAT will not ask direct questions about the meaning of words, your vocabulary will be quizzed indirectly through

reading passages and context. An understanding of how to properly use your vocabulary words on the test is essential to your success on the test.

4. **Know the material**. This one seems obvious, but often students and parents get too caught up in test-taking strategies. While it is important to know the structure of the test and the best way to maximize your points, the SSAT is, at its foundation, a test of your knowledge and logical reasoning. So know your math, know your grammar, and be able to read quickly and efficiently. No amount of tips and strategies can substitute for a strong working knowledge of the subject matter.

5. **Finally, do not get burned out!** I know I said to start studying early and often, but pace yourself. On days where you don't take a full-length practice test, limit yourself to an hour or two a day of going through practice problems you struggled with. Pacing yourself with your test prep will keep you mentally refreshed and boost your confidence when you take your SSAT.

What's the Magic Number for Your SSAT Score?

Here is the million-dollar question: what score will I need to get into a top-ten boarding school?

Well, Top Test Prep's admissions experts have compiled a list of the top boarding schools in the country.

You can find our full list here:

http://toptestprep.com/best-boarding-school-rankings

I will list the top ten schools here. Note: the average SSAT scores for admitted students do vary year to year, but bottom line, you need to score an 85th percentile or higher to be strongly considered.

1. Phillips Academy Andover

2. Phillips Exeter Academy

3. Deerfield Academy

4. St. Paul's School

5. Hotchkiss School

6. The Thacher School

7. Cate School

8. Middlesex School

9. Groton School

10. Lawrenceville School

The top two schools (Exeter and Andover) consistently have the highest SSAT percentile for admitted students. Our private school admissions experts took many different factors into account when compiling this list since we understand that you should have as much knowledge about the school as you can before making the decision on where to attend. For example, what are the average SAT scores of the graduating class, where do the graduates matriculate for college, and how much endowment does the school have for their students?

However, getting a high SSAT score will get your application considered, but it is up to the subjective part of your applications, such as your essays, interviews, and recommendations, to guarantee your admission. If you are planning to attend one of these elite boarding schools, you should have a goal score in the range of 85th to 95th percentile. To maximize your chances of getting a score in this range, you should start studying three to six months ahead of time. Take practice tests, study your vocabulary, and work on your test-taking strategies.

Five Smart Tips for ISEE Exam Prep

The Independent School Entrance Examination (ISEE) is the premier admissions test used by most private schools for students in grades five through twelve. There are three different levels of testing, depending on which grade the student is applying for, and within each of those levels, the test consists of three sections.

1. A verbal and quantitative reasoning section

2. A reading comprehension and mathematics section

3. An essay section

Here are five tips for students to use effectively as ISEE test prep methods.

1. **Time after Time**—Don't just take practice tests; time yourself as you practice. It's important to know how you will perform under the potential added pressure of being timed. After doing this a few times, you should have a good idea for the areas that you may need to work on most.

2. **Widen Your Horizons**—Sometimes the best way to prepare for the reading comprehension portion of the test is simply to immerse yourself with as much reading as you can fit into your schedule. Try a nice blend of contemporary literature with a healthy dose of the classics for the optimal widening of your reading horizons.

3. **If You Build It, It Will Come**—Your vocabulary will build if you get in the habit of looking up unfamiliar words as you read. In particular pay attention to the common uses of prefixes and suffixes as this can help you with words that maybe you haven't yet familiarized yourself with.

4. **Forget Me Not**—Sometimes it can be difficult to comprehend what you've read because you're either too tired or distracted. The best way to remember and comprehend what you're reading is to avoid reading altogether when you're in one of these states of mind. Take a break when you need to, and refresh your brain with a guilty pleasure perhaps or another favorite pastime. Maybe just picking up the phone to call a friend for a fun chat, a much-needed pick-me-up, or some words of encouragement can be all you need to get going again.

5. **Don't Procrastinate**—It's a fine line between taking a much-needed break and just flat out putting things off until the last minute. Don't let

a healthy break turn into a bad habit. Procrastination habits inevitably lead to disappointment and poor results. Get in the habit of studying early and often. You will remember more and perform better if you can balance out your study habits rather than saving them until the eleventh hour.

All about the Gateway to Prep Schools

The Gateway to Prep Schools is an online-based application for private and boarding schools, similar to the Common Application used for college. Most of the top boarding schools in the country are members of the Gateway system. You will use it to submit your entire application, from inquiry surveys to personal statements. It is convenient because you can use the same basic information, such as your candidate profiles and recommendations, and submit it to all of the schools. To have the best possible application through Gateway, follow these steps.

1. **Do not be tempted to use the same essay for different schools!** Although the Common Application uses the same main essays for all the schools, each Gateway school will require its own essay. The key to a good essay is to make it personal and tailor it to the school so that your passion is apparent in the essay. Admissions officers can tell when you recycle essays!

2. **Be thorough with your recommendations.** Make sure you have sat down with each of the people you have asked to write a recommendation for you. You want to make sure they know who you are. Your recommenders are there to help you (what teacher doesn't want to say one of their students is going to Exeter?), so don't be afraid to ask them to sit down with you.

3. **Highlight your talents.** If you are exceptional at a sport, instrument, or art, go ahead and submit supplementary materials. Be honest with yourself. Have a close friend or relative assess your abilities. You don't have to be the next Picasso or Michael Jordan, but if you participate in arts or sports just to participate, you might not want to send this stuff in. An admissions officer does not want to hear a student play chopsticks or hear from a coach that "he tries hard."

4. **Make sure your candidate profile is complete and thorough.** This may seem obvious, but you don't want a clerical error to prevent your chances of

entrance. A sloppily done candidate profile will be a huge red flag for admissions officers.

If you are planning on applying to a top boarding school, you will most likely need to familiarize yourself with the *Gateway to Prep Schools*.

Similarities between the SSAT and ISEE: What You Need to Know

The ISEE has five sections. The sections are verbal reasoning, quantitative reasoning, reading comprehension, mathematics achievement and the essay.

Here is a quick breakdown of each section.

- **Verbal reasoning** consists of synonym questions and sentence-completion questions. Synonym questions are basically a test of your vocabulary knowledge. It will give you a word and ask you to determine which response defines it most closely. Sentence-completion questions will ask you which word best completes a sentence. In both types of questions, a strong working vocabulary is key. So the best way to study for the verbal reasoning section is to study your vocabulary! Flash cards, reading books, anything to help you increase your vocabulary.

- **Quantitative reasoning** is a math section, but with word problems instead of numbers and equations. You will not be allowed to use a calculator on this section. So you should be able to think quickly and use your reasoning skills to solve these questions. The best way to study for this section is to do as many practice questions as possible so that you are familiar with all of the different types of questions that might be thrown at you.

- **Reading comprehension** is just that. You will read passages and have to answer questions based on the given passages. To study for this section, be sure that you can, first, read the passage in a reasonable amount of time and, second, understand the main idea of the passage. Helpful tips may be to write a quick summary of the passage in your own words and underline key passages as you read. Be an active reader, not a passive one.

- **Mathematics achievement** is a section that will test you on appropriate subjects for your level. On the ISEE you will be tested on basic algebra, geometry, data analysis, and numeric operations. Differing levels of the test will have different difficulties of questions in each subject.

◆ **The essay on the ISEE is not graded**, but will be submitted directly to the schools where you choose to apply. Read magazine articles and short stories to learn how to craft an organized essay with a clear introduction and conclusion. Practice on your own by picking a prompt and writing down your thoughts without interruption for 30 minutes. Edit your work by omitting unnecessary statements that are not relevant to your chosen prompt.

3 Mistakes to Avoid in Private School Admissions Essays

Private school admissions essays can seem daunting, but avoiding these most common pitfalls will get you through the process with ease. The most common mistake is when students attempt to tailor their application to show that they are the type of student the admissions committee seeks. What they often fail to realize is admissions committees have seen thousands of applications, and they are looking for unique students who have a view or passion that sets them apart from the other hundreds of applicants.

1. **Remember your (private school) audience.**
   Students often forget their target audience. As mentioned previously, the admissions committee has read hundreds of application essays, many of which are the essay the student thinks the committee wants to read. But for an essay, there is no right or wrong topic. The best essays are the ones that compel the reader to continue reading, that tell a unique story, and that pique the reader's curiosity.

2. **Choose the right topic.**
   Find your passion. Find what makes you tick, what sparks your curiosity. Is it a hobby? Is it an extracurricular? Don't be predictable. Don't write about volunteering just because you think it is the right topic. Do you play a musical instrument? Do you play a sport? What do you spend your weekends doing? Write about that topic. Passionate writing will definitely capture the admission committee's interest.

3. **Avoid clichés.**
   Don't feel compelled to start off your essay with a famous quote or end with a generic moral. Write from the heart, and write what you love about that

activity or what changed your life about that experience. A personal essay will have a much more lasting impact than a formulaic one.

How to Stand Out from Other Private School Candidates

Applying to private school can be overwhelming, and the competition for those few coveted seats is cutthroat. Therefore, it is imperative that you set yourself apart from other applicants and force the admissions committee to take note of you. The best way to do so is to show the committee what makes you unique and especially an important asset to their school.

- **Write a compelling essay.**
  Avoid predictable topics you think the admissions committee will find impressive. Instead, reflect on your interests and passions, and uncover what makes you tick. Write about that passion, hobby, or extracurricular in a personal way. Tell a story to the admissions committee that makes them decide they just have to learn more about you…by admitting you to their school!

- **Seek professional advice.**
  An educational consultant can help you find the school that is the best fit for you and guide you through the private school applications process. Finding the perfect private school can give you the edge in the application process, and an educational consultant can help you tailor your application to show the admissions committee why you are indeed an asset for their school.

- **Obtain the best recommendation letters.**
  Recommendation letters should come from people who are well connected to the school and affiliated with the school. Seek out parents of current students, alumni, or faculty who you or your family knows well, and who know you well, for the most personalized letters. Recommendation letters will only give you a competitive edge if they come from a source the school values or trusts greatly. Not every school factors in recommendation letters in the selection process, but for those that do, acquiring letters from influential sources will boost your chances of admission. An educational consultant is valuable at this step as well as she will know which schools place emphasis on recommendations in the application package.

Top Five Boarding School Admissions and Application Tips

If you're **applying to boarding schools**, there are a few quick **admissions tips** to help you navigate the private school admissions process and applications.

1. **Narrow your list of boarding schools** to ten schools at most. It's important to channel your energy into applying to fewer schools than you would when you apply to colleges or graduate schools. Further, you're younger, and the bulk of your energy shouldn't be spent on application processes, but rather on growing and learning new math and reading concepts. Additionally, keeping your boarding school list to at most ten schools (or even fewer) will allow the boarding school admissions officers to realize how serious you are about their particular school.

2. **Pick your geographic region** early in the process. You absolutely must realize that going to boarding school isn't like applying to colleges—you can easily get homesick and miss your family. Being able to visit family with a quick flight might be important to you. If, however, you're the type of student (of if you're an international student) where this isn't going to be a problem, then go ahead and apply to schools far away from home.

3. **Take your SSAT or ISEE as early as possible!** These exams could be the first set of "real" exams that you've ever had to prepare for in your short academic career. Consider getting SSAT Prep or ISEE Tutoring to help you improve your scores. After all, the SSAT and ISEE are major factors in the boarding school admissions and application process—and you need to be aware and ready to take these exams.

4. **Get a recommendation from a neighbor.** What, you might ask? How on earth could this be helpful? Well, getting a recommendation from a neighbor or community leader, could exemplify your maturity and ability to contribute to your surroundings. Remember, part of the private school application is about showing your maturity—and imagine if you have a neighbor who sees your maturity every day. Little things like this could have a significant impact

5. **Be prepared for your admissions interview!** When you're in grades five through eight, you're probably not used to interviews. In fact, if you're reading this article on boarding school admissions, I would be impressed…but the goal is to prepare for your boarding school interview by having a candid, honest conversation with a friend or family member about your goals in applying to each school. You should do research ahead of time on the applications and know more than just stuff you read on each school's website.

Public vs. Private High Schools: Which Are Better?

There are an increasing number of college admissions consultants discussing the benefits of applying to college from either a public or private high school. Further, many parents and students want to know whether going to a private high school will give them a greater advantage in the admissions cycle. We'll discuss the benefits of applying from either public or private schools.

Applying to College from Public High Schools

There's a greater chance that you might stand out more with higher SAT and ACT scores.

Most admissions offices have statistics of matriculated students from any given high school. These show the performance of students from any high school at their college. In fact, many high school admissions offices provide SAT and ACT medians from their respective school. So if you score way higher or lower, it could be seen more or less favorably.

You are more likely to be the only one applying to a top college.

Because some public high schools are more worried about students attending high school at all, if you're one of the few students applying to an Ivy League School or to another top fifty college (based on *U.S. News & World Report*), admissions officers will make note of this fact. Don't focus too much on how many students from other public high schools were accepted into Harvard. Instead, work on increasing your scores and improving your essays, and then apply to college. Don't worry about the fact that you have to apply from a public school.

Applying to College from Private High Schools

Many private schools have greater resources.

Simply put, because many private schools charge tuition and don't rely on state and local taxes to survive, private high schools can channel more resources into college counseling and other things, like computer technology. So if you're going to a private school, use the resources wisely. And our admissions consultants help both public and private school students, regardless.

There's a better chance you can speak with current and former students at top schools.

Because there are more students from private schools at the top colleges, your private school is more likely to put you in touch with a current student who can help facilitate a campus tour or discussion with the admissions office. In addition, these contacts will help you find out what school is a good fit for you. You should find out what graduates went to your choice schools and contact them.

Reminder from Ross:

Here's an important point. This book will help you get into the best private schools and boarding schools—it's up to you what you do once you gain admission. If you're the top of your class coming from a public high school, you could stand out more than if you were in the middle of the pack at a place like Phillips Exeter Academy. So don't think that the best boarding schools and private schools are guarantees to get into the best colleges—they're not. You have to work hard to distinguish yourself regardless of whether you're coming from a public or private high school.

Overall, it is doubtful that an admissions office will think any more favorably of your application whether you are coming from a public or private school. The most important thing is to create an application that shows you contributed to your high school (public or private) and will do the same in college.

Remember, the key to applying to colleges is making sure you develop a strong theme in your admissions application that shows you stood out of the crowd, regardless of whether you went to a public or private high school. Don't worry about whether you're at a public or private school, the SAT and ACT create enough objective criteria to evaluate your applications that this fact becomes irrelevant.

Why the SSAT Writing Sample Is Important

During the SSAT you will have twenty-five minutes to write a response to your choice from two prompts. There is no right or wrong answer, and the results aren't a factor in your overall score. With that said, you might be wondering why this section is on the test at all. While it isn't a scored section, the SSAT writing sample is an important indicator used by high schools to assess your creativity, communication skills, and organization of ideas. Here are some tips to provide the best writing sample possible.

- Stick to the topic, and answer the question directly. The twenty-five-minute limit isn't a lot of time, so take a few minutes to collect and organize your thoughts before jumping into the writing.

- Use specific examples. These can be personal stories, current events, or classic examples from literature or history. Wherever your interests lie, use them to provide strong support for your argument.

- Follow directions. This means write legibly, use a black pen, and follow grammar guidelines. Using a variety of relevant vocabulary words will also enliven your text.

How to Guess on the SSAT

One of the biggest dilemmas about the SSAT is whether it hurts or helps you to guess on those questions you cannot solve. First, we should discuss how the SSAT is scored. Each correct answer is worth one point. There is a guessing penalty on the SSAT, which penalizes you one-quarter of a point for each incorrect answer. This means you can get four answers wrong and break even. However, this strategy will not boost you to the top score you desire. For this, you need a better strategy than blind guesses. Here are a few tips:

If a question stumps you immediately…

Skip it and come back after you finish the section. The answers on the SSAT are designed to stem directly from the questions. If you cannot figure out how the math problem should be solved or the verbal question should be answered by reading the question, skip it and come back when you have extra time remaining to devote to it.

Use the process of elimination (POE) before guessing.

The SSAT penalizes you one-quarter of a point for each incorrect answer. However, if you are able to narrow your options down to three answer choices, the odds are in favor of guessing. At this point, having systematically eliminated two to three choices, take an educated guess before moving on.

Don't guess blindly.

The SSAT test writers are excellent at creating answer choices that resemble the correct answer. This will trap students who choose to guess when they have no idea how to solve the problem and will cost them points.

Study with a tutor.

This can help you be prepared for those trick answers, be familiar with all of the material covered on the SSAT, and avoid having to rely on guessing.

CHAPTER 7

MASTER YOUR PERSONAL STATEMENT AND ADMISSION ESSAYS

My older brother, Mike, was down in the dumps after reading a letter his girlfriend had written to break up with him. The two had dated for nearly a full year, and it was obvious Mike was disappointed their relationship was ending just before they returned to college that fall.

Our father, ever the philosopher, looked at the letter and made a quick observation.

"You know what, Mike?" Dad said. "It probably makes sense the two of you aren't together. She sounds self-centered."

After Dad took the time to make an accurate count, he noted that in the course of this one-page letter, Mike's girlfriend had written the words "I" and "me" sixty-seven times. The word "you" appeared only twice.

What does this girl dumping Mike have to do with the personal statement you submit as part of your private or boarding school application?

Well, ironically, the personal statement should not be just about you. Instead, it should mirror a love letter. A love letter from you, the suitor, to your target, the school. The letter should not brag about what you have accomplished. Instead, the personal statement is an opportunity to focus on one or two of your passions and demonstrate what you can do with these passions at the school to which you are applying. If you write "I…I…I" or "me…me…me" instead of focusing on what you can contribute to the school, the Hawk, the Scout, and the Veteran will notice.

————

When crafting your personal statement, sit down first with a pen or pencil and paper and write what comes to your mind. Don't worry about editing or having perfect structure. This is a great time to get your ideas into print so that you have an initial framework with which to work. Remember, we want to block off chunks of time over a two-week period so that the personal statement evolves into a finished product.

> **Parent tip:** I see too many of you rushing your child through this part of the process and providing your input from the beginning when it is not yet needed. This forceful nature prevents the student from finding her voice and also limits the student's ability to remain authentic. Parents need to remain patient. Let the process of writing a personal statement take its time and run its course. Use your input to influence your child and help improve each draft, but make sure this piece of writing remains the student's voice.

As with the written essays for the SSAT and ISEE, your writing should be well organized with a clear thesis, strong evidence, supporting facts, natural transitions, and an easy-to-follow conclusion.

Most personal statements are between 350 and 500 words. If your personal statement is significantly shorter than this, take some time to think things through and consider whether there are items worth adding. But, please, do not add anything simply for the sake of adding. The best writing is crisp and concise, but surely there are things you can add. The three sentences you wrote are not that epic. If your piece is much longer than 500 words, consider using an inverted pyramid format—where the most important items are at the top of the pyramid and the least important items are at the bottom—to determine where to trim. The Hawk, the Scout, and the Veteran expect your personal statement to fall in this window for length, and they budget time to read your statement based on this. You do not want to be someone with too little to contribute or someone who thinks so much of yourself than you submit a 1,500-word opus—don't laugh; I have seen this happen.

In the personal statement, your focus should be on showing your passion to the admissions committee. Remember, you want to tour the campus and interview **before** writing a personal statement. Your personal statement then should reference the visit. Personal statements are not a one-size-fits-all template where you can copy and paste things from one school to the next. Talk about how you visited a school, sat in on a class, listened to the teacher, and perhaps learned something that you had not learned in your current school. Assert that this is why you want to be part of the private or boarding school's environment and have the opportunities the school's current students enjoy. Nothing shows your interest better than having visited the school and invested your time and your energy. Your personal statement is not about how awesome you are, but how you will fit in at the school.

Myth: The personal statement is about you.

Fact: It is about your passion and what you can bring to the school.

Taking this approach will personalize your application and help set you apart from the majority of the applicant pool. I have read so many personal statements where the author fails to use this opportunity to demonstrate who she is to the admissions committee.

Topics for your personal statement can vary, but they should be consistent in one way. They should show your passion for whatever it is about which you write.

One of my favorite personal statements was most unusual, but I can say, without a doubt, it was nearly perfect. It was written by Peter, who came to us as an eighth grader interested in most of Top Test Prep's Top Ten Boarding Schools. Peter had taken control of the application process from the beginning. He had good grades, was well organized, and was operating on my preferred timeline. He had visited several campuses early in the fall and by October was working on his personal statement. Peter had top grades and excellent test scores, but where he stood apart was in his reading. It is conservative to say that Peter had read twice as many books as his peers. He was interested in all genres.

For his personal statement, Peter decided to take a chance. He took Ernest Hemingway's famous book *The Old Man and the Sea* and wrote how he felt like Hemingway as he went through the boarding school application process. Peter talked about being out on the ocean, searching for the big catch and the big fish; he said that he loved fishing but that his current school did not provide the opportunity for him to fish. Peter was so passionate, getting right into the characters and taking the reader aboard Hemingway's boat in the middle of this vast body of water. A passionate writer takes the reader to the scene of the crime, and that is what Peter did in fewer than five hundred descriptive words.

Peter's personal statement was so simple that it was fantastic. Not only did the writing show that he was well read and familiar with this mature literature, but it also allowed him to connect with his passion and share what he would do with it when he got to that school. Equally important, it was Peter's voice—not his parent's. With that level of maturity, don't you think a student like Peter would add value at Andover or Exeter, where an English teacher has a class of seven kids talking about a book? Of course he would. Finally, by taking the chance with a personal statement that was outside the norm, Peter showed that he was willing to try something new that might be outside his comfort zone—much like boarding students are required to do on a regular basis at their new school. Admissions officers are on the lookout for students willing to try new things with the same passion that they have shown for things they already have done. This essay was so much better than if Peter had simply written about his interest in literature and all of the books he had read and why he had read them.

It was one of the most powerful personal statements I have ever read. It was no surprise that Peter went to Exeter.

Myth: Use the personal statement to make yourself sound as great as possible. List everything you have done to showcase your qualifications.

Fact: Focus on your passion, which will help make a connection with the admissions officers who read your application.

Regardless of whether your personal statement is as innovative as Peter's, you still can find ways to display your passion and convey this passion to the reader. If you are a terrific violin player, show how you became such a great violinist on your own volition, not how your parents pushed you to take up the violin. That shows a level of maturity. Don't twist the truth, but be sure to accentuate the parts of the story you find most important. Just like the car salesman does not point out a slight dent in a bumper, you can gloss over the fact that your parents wanted you to take up the violin and instead focus on the dedication shown by your weekly lessons. This is an opportunity to build your own theme, so take advantage of it.

Here are some guidelines to follow when writing your personal statement.

- **Be authentic.** Make sure the writing is your own voice and that the thoughts and feelings are yours as well. There needs to be consistency between your personal statement and your interview with an admissions representative. If you do not believe what you wrote, there is the potential for trouble.

- **Read the finished product out loud to your parents and friends.** Read carefully. Don't just read what you meant to write, read what is in print. You will find grammar mistakes, typos, and dropped words. Just as important, you will know if the writing sounds like your voice or whether it is too formal and loaded with SAT-type words. Well-written pieces are conversational in tone. You want your writing to read the same as if you were holding a conversation with the reader.

- **Write about your passion.** There are a million permutations of topics and ways to write your personal statement. You need to write about your passions and not be afraid to be emotional—like Julie was with soccer in Chapter 3. You need to build a theme so that between your personal statement and your interview, the admissions committee gets to know you. Be candid. If you are funny, let that show, too.

There are also things to avoid. Here are three types of all-too-common personal statements that leave the Hawk, the Scout, and the Veteran shaking their heads.

- **Don't write that you are going to save the world.** Even if you are the most optimistic, selfless teenager ever, save it for your interview with an admissions representative. The Hawk, the Scout, and the Veteran will roll their eyes if you send this in as your personal statement.

- **Don't write that you want to go to an elite school because your family is wealthy, and, by the way, when you get to the campus you feel badly for poor people and you are going to help poor people.** Guess what—most of the people applying to these schools come from means. That is just the way it is, and you do not have to apologize for it. Besides, if you were committed to helping poor people, you could show this by writing about things you already have accomplished, such as the coat drive you organized at your school last winter or the three hours you volunteer every Saturday morning helping recent Spanish-speaking immigrants learn English.

- **Don't write a list of all the things you have done.** It is not authentic and is just a redundant mention of all of your extracurricular activities. Remember, you should focus your personal statement on the one or two things about which you are most passionate.

When I was in middle school, I had two passions: classical literature, notably Homer's epics the Odyssey and the Iliad, and history, particularly World War I. Fascinated by understanding how one-time events can shape the evolution of society and politics, I was consumed by learning about the assassination of Archduke Franz Ferdinand of Austria and how his death started World War I. Going to boarding school presented the opportunity to discuss these topics more openly and be well-received, something that was much harder to do in a small Texas town, as much as

I loved my hometown and still do. While it is unlikely you have the same passions I did, this speaks to the importance of finding your voice and showing your passion. When the Hawk, the Scout, and the Veteran at NMH in the mid-1990s read my personal statement, they knew they were getting a student who was going to challenge his teachers and peers in the classroom.

Writing tip: After you have read the piece out loud, go back to your computer and go word-by-word to see if it is possible to make your writing tighter. Treat each word as a valuable piece of real estate—you only have a limited amount to use. Just like a private or boarding school needs every student to contribute to its community, you need every word to make a difference in your writing.

See what words can be deleted. Look for phrases that can be made shorter. Make sure your adjectives are descriptive and your verbs are active. You want the Hawk, the Scout, and the Veteran to be able to picture what you are writing. For example, if you are writing about your passion for cooking, describe how you love the aromas that permeate from a kitchen and how you get goose bumps as you crack an egg and it sizzles in a frying pan. I do not like to use adverbs—everyone has their own style, and you will develop yours.

You will be amazed how easy it is to edit your writing and make it come to life—after years of classwork where teachers do everything they can to compel students to be wordy. Think about it: when was the last time you had an assignment where the length was not dictated by pages? So what do you do? When you are a few lines short of completing an assigned two-page report, do you perform more research or look for another source? If you do this, you are in a select club—almost no students take this route! Most likely, you add a few words here, a few more there, replace a word with a four-syllable SAT word and maybe try to get another line or two by playing with the margins or spacing. Right?

> After reading this, I hope you take the former option and do more work. When writing a two-page paper, you should have enough information to fill three or more pages. If you need to trim your writing, you can then turn to the inverted pyramid and lop off the items at the bottom. Not only will this impact the personal statement and supplemental essays for your private and boarding school applications, this also will take your schoolwork to another level. I guarantee that your teachers will notice the difference.

Another of my favorite personal statements came from a former student, Katie, who wrote about how her family had moved across the country when she was five and the impact it had on her childhood. Forget about the choice of subject—as we discussed previously, the range of topics about which you might write is vast, and the Hawk, the Scout, and the Veteran do not grade you on your topic.

What impressed me most about Katie was her writing style and word choice; both were well beyond her years. She had completed her applications by the time she came to Top Test Prep and wanted our help shaping her essays as she applied to Cate and Thacher, a pair of boarding schools in California. Katie's grades were solid, but not spectacular. However, her application was enhanced by her extracurricular activities and a devotion to hiking and camping. She was president of her school's Outdoors Club and helped lead programs for younger children at local parks.

The best part about Katie's personal statement is that it meshed with her personality and interests. She wrote about how she "explored" her new neighborhood and remembered being "distinctly impressed by a woodsy park that stood out starkly against the concrete jungle that surrounded it." Her language was terrific—colorful and descriptive. When I read this, I imagined the scene—which is what you have to do for the admissions committee.

Katie could have made her writing tighter and more fine-tuned. She could have deleted the words distinctly and starkly, which only reiterate the words they are modifying.

Still, in a short amount of space, Katie displayed an extensive vocabulary and the ability to know when to use words that are not used every day.

Her **X-factor** resonated throughout her personal statement. The writing was not about how her family had uprooted and moved, but rather on the impact it made on Katie's life and how it forever changed her as a person.

Myth: "How I can save the world" is a strong topic for your personal statement on how you want to use your education at an elite school.

Fact: Save yourself and the admissions officers the trouble of reading a trite essay with little substance. If you are that interested in saving the world, you already performed tangible deeds that show your passion.

*** Supplemental Essays ***

Each supplemental essay should run about 250 words. Although half the length of your personal statement, your supplemental essays should follow the same guidelines for organization and style. With space limited, your word choice becomes even more important.

The subjects of these essays will vary from school to school. Some of the basic ones might be similar to the following:

* Why are you a good match for our school?

* What can you bring to our class?

With these questions your focus should be on continuing the narrative created with your personal statement—and staying away from the things to avoid in the personal statement, shared on my list. These essays provide another outlet to show your passion and connect it to the school. Write about how you have thrived in settings with smaller groups. Or write about the satisfaction you derive from being challenged by your peers, which you anticipate will happen on a daily basis at a private or boarding school.

There are also eclectic supplemental essay questions such as the following:

- What was the biggest failure with which you have had to deal?

- What was your happiest moment?

With these types of the questions, you should reflect on situations you have encountered and focus on the lessons you have learned from these moments. You do not want to recite the facts, but rather delve into the emotion and look forward to what might happen if you find yourself in similar circumstances.

Regardless of the topic, the supplemental essays should be used as a method of providing context for your interest in a particular school. Use this space to make the point that this school is the right place for you.

Contrast Katie's word choice with this supplemental question a former student, Marcus, brought to us in his initial application to Groton when asked, "What makes you laugh out loud?"

> *The monkeys at the zoo make me laugh out loud because they have no sense of societal etiquette. When I see monkeys, it makes me think of what humans would be like if we hadn't gotten so smart.*

I still cringe when reading this. For starters the response was limited to 750 characters. We can easily trim 30 characters because Marcus repeated the question at the beginning of his essay, something he did in multiple responses. He should have started it this way:

> *The monkeys at the zoo because…*

Next, Marcus used the word "societal" where he meant to say "social." Marcus is from Singapore, but he had studied in the United States for two years before returning to Singapore for eighth grade and then applying to elite boarding schools. On its own, a foreign student using the word incorrectly would not be a big deal, but combined with a lack of editing, this showed a lack of motivation to fill out the application as well as possible.

In his supplemental questions, Marcus wrote that he loved "the athletic competitiveness of my school, particularly in rugby" and that "my school is one of my favorite places to be because it offers challenging classes, as well as a diverse range of extracurricular activities." But then when asked what he liked about Groton, Marcus wrote this:

> *Groton presents me with interesting opportunities that I presently do not have, sports and academic wise. In Singapore I can take part in Rugby and Cross country but they don't have a crew team. At Groton I will be able to pursue Cross-country and be able to try new ones such as crew. I would also be interested in rounding up part of the student body and creating a new rugby team for the school to share my athletic passion with other students.*

Confused? I was, too. Marcus had mentioned his passion for rugby and then said that Groton would present him with new opportunities in athletics when Groton does not have a rugby team. I give Marcus credit for saying he wants to take the initiative and start a rugby team at Groton, but in general what he writes is not consistent. Also, there are punctuation and grammar mistakes. I have no idea why rugby and cross-country are capitalized while crew is not. In another essay, Marcus wrote about needing to give "110 percent," which is one of the oldest clichés in sports and something that is not possible.

Writing tip: Stay away from clichés at all costs. Be original. Use your own words.

When reading Marcus's application, it felt as if I was reading the work of a child who was being forced into this process by his parents and had yet to take responsibility for it. This is not the impression you want to make on the Hawk, the Scout, and the Veteran.

Writing tip: If you use material that is not original, be certain to always cite your source. If you paraphrase something and are not sure whether you need to provide credit, do it. Always. Citing a source will never count against you, but failing to do so can kill your chances of admission. In this day and age, when it is easy for the Hawk, the Scout, and the Veteran to check your text to see if you have copied and pasted someone else's work, it is foolish to not take this simple step.

———

There are few hard rules to follow when writing your personal statement and supplemental essays. What works for one person might not for another. The most important thing is to be yourself. These pieces should be extensions of your interview with the admissions committee and help them get to know you better.

Look at Katie. Normally, I would never advise writing about an event that happened eight years ago, before she was even in kindergarten. The best topics are fresher in your mind, usually tied to something in the past year or two.

But this huge move was a defining event in Katie's life. That park was her sanctuary, "a silent memorial erected to honor my most treasured childhood memories." Notice how Katie's word choice remains exceptional. Ever heard a park talk before? But describing the park as "a silent memorial" is an excellent description. I picture the boulders on which she climbed and a quiet solitude interrupted only by the chirping of birds throughout the park.

Contrast that with Marcus's writing. He was very matter-of-fact, lacked descriptive words, and needed to work with a strong editor who could help turn his plain Jane answers into responses that provided insight into who he was. Fortunately for Marcus, we were able to match him with one of our top tutors and improve his writing. He ended up getting into Exeter and The Hun School.

CHAPTER 8

THE BRAG SHEET (IT'S OK TO BRAG!)

Don't laugh at the title of this chapter.

One of the mistakes most people make throughout life is underselling themselves. They are too humble or assume that people with whom they are acquainted know all about them.

Students, in particular, are guilty of this. They are not accustomed to self-promotion and have heard plenty of talk about not having too much of an ego—especially those near the top of their classes who already stand out at a young age.

At Top Test Prep, we developed the Brag Sheet as a template for students to highlight their activities and accomplishments to the people they are asking for recommendations to boarding and private schools.

Face it, people are always being told to stay humble. Well, the Brag Sheet is the one opportunity to boast about yourself. You will list your achievements inside and outside the classroom year by year. You will write about your future plans and goals. Then you will take the Brag Sheet to each teacher you are asking for a recommendation because—guess what?—your teachers don't know as much about you as you think. You might assume that because you are Mrs. Johnson's favorite student in science, she knows everything you have done for the past three years. But even if you have had plenty of after-class talks and shared stories from your personal life, Mrs. Johnson will be hard pressed to remember these. She just knows you are well behaved in class each day for forty-five minutes and get As on all of your assignments.

The Brag Sheet is a way to make sure your teachers know you and see your passion.

Don't worry about coming across as conceited. No teacher is going to think you are a terrible person for doing this.

Myth: Stay humble. You don't want to look like an egomaniac.

Fact: This is your one chance to brag and explain why your achievements are important. This is not a paper that will be graded. It is a cheat sheet for your recommender to be able to write a letter that makes an impact.

The formula for the Brag Sheet is simple:

- List your accomplishments in school for each of the past three or four years. List each item with a bullet point, and describe it in detail. There is no such thing as providing too much information in this space.
    - Be sure to name the school that you attended each year and where it is located.
    - Mention your GPA or grades if they are beneficial. For instance, of course you want our recommendation letter to mention that you earned straight As in seventh grade. But would you want the letter to mention that you were a B student in middle school?
    - List the years in reverse chronological order, so that the most recent events are at the top. This is staying with our inverted pyramid format, where we want the most important things first

- List your most noteworthy achievements outside of school. This section can include the following:
    - Hobbies
    - Athletics
    - Foreign languages you speak
    - Travel
    - Volunteering and community service programs

Again, it is important here to use your judgment. Remember, quality over quantity. You are not looking to create a never-ending list here, but rather a few top items that will make an impact. The sole purpose of the Brag Sheet is to make a recommendation letter easier for a teacher to write and have it include the information you want the Hawk, the Scout, and the Veteran to read. Be certain to put each item into context. If you won the US Tennis Association's twelve-and-under national championship, say so—and be sure to note what a player has to do to participate in the event, how many players qualified, and where it was held.

- List any summer programs, jobs, or internships you have held, describing your duties and responsibilities and what you learned from each position.
  - Include the impact you made.
  - Mention any promotions or honors you received, such as Employee of the Month.

- List your future plans.

- Wrap up the Brag Sheet by providing a list of schools to which you are applying, when the recommendation letter needs to be submitted, and how to submit it.

The Brag Sheet is not a complicated piece of work, but this one- or two-page document performs a Herculean task of providing information to the teachers you ask for recommendations. You want to go into as much detail as possible when writing your Brag Sheet, as teachers will rely on this when they write your recommendations. And when a recommendation goes into detail, it creates the perception that the teacher knows the student well and makes a bigger impact.

With each of these—except for the list of schools where you will apply—keep your lists to no more than three items. Just like in your personal statements and supplemental essays, it is a matter of quality over quantity. If you list too many things, they will get lost in the shuffle and you will be asking the recommender to decide which items are most important instead of telling the recommender what is important. Also, if these items continue a theme, it will contribute even more to showing your passion, which is the goal for your recommendation letters. If you begin compiling your Brag Sheet and find that you have too many items, create an inverted pyramid, and use your judgment to decide which are most important. Also, on each list, the most important item should go at the top.

For example, if I had written a Brag Sheet for myself, my entries for seventh grade would have included items like these:

- Second place, Junior Optimist Society of Northeast Texas speech competition. Public speaking competition before an auditorium of four hundred people, with thirty students making speeches. Gave a speech about the biggest challenges facing our seniors including health care problems.

- Honorable mention in the University Interscholastic League state of Texas championship Spelling Bee. Competed in regional competitions. Placed in the top ten in the regional championship spelling bee. Yes, I love reading, writing, and the all the joys of spelling!

These events would have been in line with my desire to show myself as an intellectual in search of a more challenging academic environment than what I had in Texarkana. When the NMH admissions officers reviewed my application and recommendation letters, would they have known anything about the Junior Optimist Society of Northeast Texas or the University Interscholastic League? Probably not. My middle school teachers would have been hard pressed to know much about the Junior Optimist Society, though everyone in Texarkana knew about the University Interscholastic League, which is the state sanctioning body for high school athletics and activities in Texas. Still, if a teacher read these items on my Brag Sheet, she would have the context for each item. One was a public speaking competition, the other a spelling bee. The short descriptions give my recommenders the ability to write about these events on a personal basis.

This is information that all recommenders will use in their letters on your behalf. Your job is to make the recommendation letter as easy as possible for the teacher to write—providing this information will accomplish this goal.

Don't be afraid to "humbly" boast about yourself.

Myth: Some achievements are self-explanatory and do not require description.

Fact: You can never go into too much detail. The more details you provide, the better you will be.

Brag Sheet Template

Accomplishments in School

Eighth Grade

- Example: Champion skier

Seventh Grade

- Example:

Sixth Grade

- Example:

Fifth Grade

- Example:

Accomplishments outside of School

- Example: Awards, etc.

Summer Programs, Internships, and Jobs

- Example:

Future Plans/Goals

Example: Writing novels, attending business school

I'm applying to these prep schools:

Deadline for Recommendation:

How to Submit (Online/Mail To):

———

The Brag Sheet is not meant to be a drawn-out exercise. Rather, it is a one- or two-page document that promotes the student. Too many boarding and private applicants undersell themselves—even those that are motivated enough to come to Top Test Prep to help them with the application process.

Let's look at a two sample Brag Sheets as completed by the students.

Jonathan Williams' Brag Sheet

Accomplishments in School

Seventh Grade at Suburban Middle School in Rockville, Maryland:

* Earned straight As in both semester.

* Placed second in the IBM Science Fair.

* Captain the boys' tennis team.

Sixth Grade at Suburban Middle School in Rockville, Maryland:

* Earned straight As in both semesters.

* Named most respectful Student.

* Played No. 2 singles on the boys' tennis team.

Fifth Grade at Redbrick Elementary School:

* Earned five As and one B in each semester.

* Played piano in the school recital and earned the "Most Improved Award."

* Captain of the school safety patrols.

Accomplishments Outside of School

* Tae Kwon Do black belt.

* Volunteered at Martha's Table.

* Won the Mid-Atlantic Tennis Association 14-and-under boys' singles championship and qualified for the US tennis association championship in Miami in August.

Summer Programs and Jobs

* June 2012-present: Pro shop assistant and racket stringer at Chevy Chase Club in Chevy Chase, Maryland.

* July 2013: Attended the National Student leadership Conference at American university. Took a course in speech writing.

Future Plans/Goals

* I would like to earn a college scholarship.

* I plan to attend an Ivy League school and major in biology.

I am applying to these prep schools: Blair, Pedie, Deerfield, Exeter.

What are the first things you notice? I was stunned by the occasional misspelled word, incorrect capitalization, poor grammar, and even the misspelling of one of the schools to which Jonathan was applying, Peddie. The lack of attention to detail makes it hard for a teacher to have the desire to write glowing things for Jonathan's recommendation. Remember, no recommendation is going to be negative, but there are many degrees of positive recommendations.

Furthermore, and even worse than these typographical errors, Jonathan provided absolutely no context for any of his achievements. When he takes his Brag Sheet to his teachers, how much will they learn about Jonathan? Will they get to know him on an intimate level? Jonathan is missing the opportunity to share his passion with his teachers and solidify his connection with them. He needs to take the time to flesh out each item and provide details that his teachers can use to supplement their recommendations.

Finally, while Jonathan provided a list of schools to which he is applying, he did not set a date for the recommendations to be submitted or provide instructions for submitting the recommendations. What if one of the schools has an early application deadline or if one of his teachers waits until mid-February to write the letter? Even if Jonathan provided this information in a separate e-mail to his recommenders, he should include it here as well so they do not have to keep track of this information or go look for it later. Remember, the goal of the Brag Sheet is to make things as easy as possible for the recommenders.

Jonathan's Brag Sheet still was helpful, as it does provide information that his teachers probably do not know. However, to take advantage of the Brag Sheet, Jonathan needed to put in more time and boast about his accomplishments.

Jane Smith's Brag Sheet

Accomplishments in School

Seventh Grade at Suburban Middle School in Rockville, Maryland:

- While taking four honors courses (math, English, science, history), earned straight As in both semesters for the second consecutive year. One of only two students in the three-hundred-person school to get straight As for the entire school year.

- Won second place in the IBM Mid-Atlantic Regional Science Fair with a research project titled "Snowy Broken Roads: How the Washington Area Can Avoid Having So Many Potholes." More than fifty individual school science fair winners qualified for this prestigious event.

- Captain of the school girls' tennis team, the first seventh grader ever to captain the team. Playing No. 1 singles won all ten of my matches and spent considerable practice time helping my teammates improve so we could win our first league championship in twenty-five years.

Sixth Grade at Suburban Middle School in Rockville, Maryland:

- While taking honors English and honors math, earned straight As in both semesters, one of five students in the three-hundred-person school to accomplish this feat.

- Earned most respectful student in my one-hundred-person class, as voted on by staff and teachers.

- Played No. 2 singles on the girls' tennis team and won all but one of my ten matches. Was the only sixth grader in the school to make the team.

Fifth Grade at Redbrick Elementary School in Houston, Texas:

- Earned five As and one B in each semester, the highest grades of any student in my twenty-five-person class.

- Played piano in the school recital and earned the "Most Improved Award" from our teacher. It was my first time ever playing a musical instrument outside of class.

- Captain of the school safety patrols. In my third year as a patrol, I was responsible for helping to oversee the twenty-person program, making sure there were enough student volunteers and that each knew their duty before and after school. For the first time in three years, there was not one safety incident for Redbrick students as they went to and from school.

Accomplishments outside of School

- This past June won the Mid-Atlantic Tennis Association fourteen-and-under girls' singles championship. The tournament was held in Richmond, Virginia, and had sixty-four entries. By winning the tournament, I qualified for the US Tennis Association championship in Miami in August, where I won my first two matches and advanced to the third round before losing in three sets to the eventual champion.

- Earned Tae Kwon Do black belt and used my training to help tutor elementary school girls interested in self defense.

- Volunteered on Saturday mornings at Martha's Table, a neighborhood homeless shelter that also provides social services to members of the community in need. Helped serve breakfast every weekend. Arrived by seven o'clock to help prepare food, then served the meal and stayed until eleven, working to clean up the dining room. I found satisfaction in helping others, but even more importantly my time there showed me not to take for granted everything that I have.

Summer Programs and Jobs

- June 2012–present: Pro shop assistant and racket stringer at Chevy Chase Club in Chevy Chase, Maryland. Work twenty hours each week in the pro shop, helping members purchase apparel and rackets. Also string tennis, racquetball, and squash rackets. Have implemented several measures aimed at making the shop more cost efficient and environmentally friendly, such as dimmed lighting during nonpeak hours and instituting a recycling program for worn shoes.

- July 2013: Attended the National Student Leadership Conference at American University. One of two students from my school selected to attend this prestigious two-week overnight program. Took a course in speech writing, and in the fall made a presentation at a school assembly on what I learned so my classmates could benefit from my participation.

Future Plans/Goals

- I would like to continue to improve as a tennis player and earn a college scholarship.

- I plan to attend an Ivy League school and major in biology. My father and his father were dentists, and I would like to join their practice.

I am applying to these prep schools: Blair, Peddie, Deerfield, Exeter.

Please submit your recommendation by October 15.

I have attached stamped and addressed envelopes to each recommendation or you can e-mail them to each school's admissions office: admission@blair.edu, admission@peddie.org, admission@deerfield.edu, and admit@exeter.edu.

Jane's list of accomplishments was identical to Jonathan's. However, with each item, Jane provided great context. She rattled off specific names, dates, and locations for events. She quantified how many entrants were in different competitions. She gave the title of her science fair project and described what it was. This information is perfect for a teacher using Jane's Brag Sheet as a guideline for writing a recommendation.

Look at the items in Jane's Brag Sheet. Each year, there is one item for her academic accomplishments. There are also items that show her interest in athletics and helping others. And each time, Jane provides great context, talking about how she did, what she learned and the impact she made. She did not include trivial items, and each of her bullet points seems like a big deal. Your Brag Sheet need not be all about grades or academic honors, and it can include anything that shows passion. If Julie, who we met in Chapter 3, had put together a Brag Sheet, it would have included plenty of information about her soccer career.

Myth: Your favorite teachers know all about you. They call on you during class, and you stay after class to chat for a few minutes, so they will have no problem writing the perfect recommendation letter for you.

Fact: You are one of one hundred students to them. Even if they do know all about you—and can remember this information while writing their recommendation letter—you should make things as easy as possible for them and provide reminders about what you have accomplished and your passion.

After reading Jonathan's Brag Sheet and Jane's Brag Sheet, is there any doubt which student would receive better recommendation letters?

Not all applicants will be as accomplished as Jane, but everyone can show the same level of passion.

Parent tip: Help your children remember everything they have accomplished and realize the significance of each accomplishment. Students tend to see the world only through their own eyes. Let your children benefit from your experience. You are closer in age to the members of the admissions committee, so let your children know what an adult might consider important or less important.

CHAPTER 9

HOW TO GET THE BEST TEACHER RECOMMENDATIONS

My favorite teacher in seventh grade was Mrs. Day. She was a tall woman in her sixties who, for some reason, appreciated that I loved broadening my vocabulary. Mrs. Day never minded if I used long words during class or in reports describing various pieces of literature I had read. It was a rare moment in my day when I did not worry about being embarrassed by not conforming to how my peers went about their schoolwork.

Each night I would learn a new word, and I looked forward to going to her class the next day and tossing out this new word. I was one of the few students who spoke during each day's discussion period. I stayed after class at least three times a week to further talk about what we were learning. While I shied away from sharing my thoughts in the classroom with other students, I talked freely with Mrs. Day, who was six feet tall but seemed even taller because I had yet to hit my growth spurt.

But while Mrs. Day and I had a connection in class each day for fifty minutes, did she know anything about what I was like when I left her in classroom?

Yes, Mrs. Day knew I had near-perfect grades, and she likely also knew I got in trouble for being a loudmouth and getting into fights with other boys.

However, Mrs. Day had no way of knowing that I grew up with my single father and older brother. And while based on my grades and extensive vocabulary, she could have guessed our family emphasized education, there was no chance she could know that the impetus for this was that my father wanted to do better than his father, a factory worker who did not even attend high school. Mrs. Day did not know that I was fascinated by World War II and wanted to know everything about this world-changing event from start to finish. She did not know that I had to hide many of my interests from my closest friends for fear they would not accept me. She did not even know I was a competitive speller or that I finished second in the Junior Optimist Society's speech competition.

In short, while Mrs. Day was at the top of my list of teachers to ask for a recommendation to boarding school, she only knew English Class Ross or maybe even Middle School Ross. She had no clue about Whole Ross.

My job, when asking her for a letter of recommendation, was to make sure she knew me well enough so she could convey this to the Hawk, the Scout, and the Veteran.

Now, when I counsel students and their families on the application process, too many times I hear students say their science teacher, Mr. Howell, or their social studies teacher, Mrs. Bluejeans, knows everything about them and will write the best recommendation. Instantly, I shake my head and make sure my students know one of the oldest rules in the books:

Rule #1: Do not assume anything. Do you know the old saying about what happens when you *assume* something? You make an *ass* out of *you* and *me*. Well, it holds true here, too.

Sure, you might have a great relationship with Mr. Howell. He calls on you in class, and you are one of two or three students who linger after class to discuss each day's lesson. It seems that he values your opinion and contributions. This is great, as you want to be able to approach a teacher with whom you have connected.

Do not assume that your favorite teacher knows everything about you. In fact, quite the opposite. Assume that this teacher knows **nothing** about you. Your job, much like I had to do with Mrs. Day, is to provide as much information as possible for the teacher to write the best possible recommendation.

Do not confuse your teacher-student relationship with Mr. Holmes with him knowing everything about you. Does he know you are the soccer team's best player or that you have been playing a clarinet solo in your renowned church choir for the past five years? Doubtful, even if your name is a regular on the morning announcements. Your teachers never know as much about you as you think they do. Your charge is to make sure they do know all about you prior to writing their recommendation and that they understand the purpose of their recommendation.

> Myth: Teachers understand the logistics of writing the recommendation. Once you ask them to write the letter, they can handle it from there.
>
> Fact: Even if a teacher can take care of everything without assistance, they will appreciate your interest in making things as easy as possible for them. Hold their hand, and provide every little detail of what needs to be done.

Every student applying to private and boarding schools gets teacher recommendations. And you know what? Every one of these recommendations is positive and talks about how great the student is. In all my years dealing with admissions and working with Top Test Prep, I have yet to hear about a less-than-glowing recommendation. If there were the slightest chance a teacher would write something negative, what student would go to that teacher for a recommendation?

This is just like our X-Factor chart in Chapter 3, where we discussed having good grades and SSAT or ISEE scores and the fact that these items will not assure your admittance but that bad grades and scores will harm your chances for admission. In this case the entire applicant pool has positive teacher recommendations that read the same, so for these students there is no benefit. The applicants for whom the recommendations will make an impact have recommendations that combine with the interview, personal statement, and supplemental essays to let the Hawk, the Scout, and the Veteran continue to get to know the student.

A recommendation letter stresses this in three ways.

1. How you stand out from your peers.

2. How you show passion about topics and come up with new information while your peers stick to textbooks.

3. How you communicate, particularly your ability to share your hopes and dreams. If a student has in mind what she would like to be in the future—be it a doctor, writer, whatever—a teacher will relate to that.

———

By the time you start thinking about teacher recommendations, your Brag Sheet should be complete, as we discussed in Chapter 6. Next, consider what teachers know you best. Sit down with your parents to go over the possibilities and narrow the choices. These do not have to be your most recent teachers or the teachers who gave you As. Instead, these should be teachers with whom you have a connection and who are willing to put in a small amount of time to help you, such as the science teacher who devoted hours to helping with your project that won second place in the school science fair or the French teacher who organized the tutoring sessions you participated in for the French immersion program at the nearby elementary school.

Parent tip: When having this conversation, ask your child who her favorite teacher is and what teachers have sparked her interest. The purpose is twofold. First, you want the recommender to be a teacher who can write coherently about your child. Second, you want a recommender who is invested in your child and will go the extra mile to help your child succeed. The best recommenders are teachers with whom your child has connected and who know how your child contributes in a classroom setting.

———

Here are some frequently asked questions:

How many recommendations should you have?

You should have three recommendations. This is a number that allows you to ask only teachers with whom you have a strong relationship and provides some depth for the admissions committee to get to know you.

What teachers should you ask for a recommendation?

Some schools and the "Gateway to Prep Schools" specify recommendations from one or two specific teachers, especially English. For the other recommendations, it does not matter which teachers you ask, though few students will ask their math teachers for these "at-large" recommendations, as math is not a subject that lends itself to teachers and students getting to know each other on a more personal level.

Unlike colleges, which have strict formulas for recommendations, boarding and private schools are more open and adaptive as they know there are a multitude of potential teachers who know you best. They are looking for recommendations that demonstrate the applicant has a certain level of maturity. This does not mean they are looking for some kid who dresses up in a suit and tie and is the most professional kid in the world. As we have discussed throughout this book, the Hawk, the Scout, and the Veteran are always on the lookout for students who stand out from their peers and lead the discussion in class.

Is there a statute of limitations for asking a teacher for a recommendation?

Yes. Limit your recommendations to teachers whose classes you have taken in the previous two years. Also, if possible, do not ask grade school teachers for recommendation letters, as two years is a significant period of time for you to change. If you are applying to matriculate as a ninth grader, you are a much different person as an eighth grader than you were as a fifth grader. If you are applying to middle schools or elite private day schools such as Trinity or Horace Mann, then you have to go back to your grade school teachers, though they will not be able to attest to your maturity level because of your age when they taught you.

How should you ask a teacher for her recommendation?

After deciding which teachers you will ask for recommendations, you need to approach them properly. This does not mean going up to them just before the bell rings to start class or even trying to use the five minutes between classes to broach the subject. Don't do it during lunch—which is a precious time for a teacher, often the only break they get all day. Instead, find a moment to tell the teacher you are applying to a new school for the following year and would like to ask for their recommendation and set up a separate meeting to discuss this. You are asking the teacher to go out of her way for you, so do it on their schedule. Remember, the best recommendations are personalized and make the student stand out. You want the teachers you ask to do this for you, so you should be willing to accommodate them.

Myth: Teachers understand why you are asking them to write a recommendation letter.

Fact: These letters are unique, and many teachers are never asked to do this. Explain to the teacher what you are doing, why you want to attend another school, and why you are asking her to write a recommendation letter on your behalf.

What should you take to the meeting with the teacher to discuss her recommendation?

You should take four things to this meeting:

◆ Brag Sheet

◆ List of schools to which you are applying

◆ The application deadlines for each school, as well as a date by which you would like each recommendation sent

◆ Instructions on how to send the recommendation letters to each school

Remember, you want to make things as easy as possible for the recommender. The Brag Sheet highlights your accomplishments and provides information you would like the recommender to share in her letter. You want the recommender to know where you are applying—maybe the recommender has a connection to one or more of these schools and is willing to reach out on your behalf.

Also, because your job is to make the process seamless, you should provide each recommender with links to submit the recommendations online and envelopes that are addressed and have postage so the recommendations can be mailed to the schools if the teacher prefers.

Should you ask to review the recommendation letter before it is sent?

While there is a curiosity to see what a recommender writes about you, as a rule of thumb, you should expect to never see these letters. Waive any rights to review the recommendation. If a teacher wants to show you the recommendation ahead of time, of course, take the opportunity. But rest assured that no teacher is going to write anything bad about you.

What should you say to the teacher when you ask for her recommendation?

When I went to Mrs. Day to ask for her recommendation, my body tingled with goose bumps. I felt guilty and was afraid of being perceived as the guy who thought he was too good for his school. After all, I was in Texarkana, where few kids even knew what a boarding school was. It was only years later, as I counseled students about this process, that I realized there was no need to be nervous. Nearly all teachers are in their profession because they take great pride and satisfaction in helping students and want the best for them. Mrs. Day was honored that I asked for her recommendation—and your teachers will feel the same way.

When you meet with a teacher to ask for a recommendation, explain why you are interested in a private or boarding school. **Don't** say that your parents are making you do this; instead you want to be seen as someone who is spearheading this process. **Don't** get caught saying that your current school is not good enough or providing enough of a challenge—you do not want to offend a teacher who will then think you believe you are too good for her class. Explain to your teacher that going to a different school provides different opportunities or that you are looking for a new environment in which you can thrive. Your focus here should be on new opportunities, traveling, and seeing new things.

Remember, few teachers have a strong knowledge of private and boarding schools, especially teachers at public schools in the South and West. In the United States, less than 1 percent of schoolchildren attend boarding schools. Applying to boarding schools is unusual, so take time to explain to your teachers why you are doing this. Often, an applicant's parents or families have a connection to a school.

Ask the recommender to focus on describing you as a person and how you would do on your own. Boarding schools want to know about your maturity. Private schools want to know if you are a leader among peers and how you kick ass in school.

Also, ask your teacher to write the recommendation on school letterhead. While this is not a big deal and not always possible, every bit helps, and a recommendation on letterhead will look better.

Be sure to give your teacher plenty of time to write the recommendation letter. The teacher needs time to read your Brag Sheet, think about the conversation the two of you have in your meeting and ponder your contributions to class. You do not want the teacher to do a rush job—it will show. Also, ask the teacher to submit the recommendation well in advance of any deadline, and later check back with the teacher to see if the letter has been submitted. If for some reason the teacher has forgotten to submit the recommendation, there is still time for the teacher to take care of it.

Parent tip: Discuss with your child the process of asking for recommendations, but do not contact your child's teachers who will be writing recommendations. You do not want to be viewed by the teachers as an overbearing parent and, conversely, it is important for your child to be seen as taking control of the application process.

There is no set length for a recommendation letter. It can be as short as two or three concise paragraphs. Or it can be more than multiple pages, though these run the risk of appearing inauthentic and not believable. The best recommendation letters, as I mentioned above, contribute to our overall goal of using the application to let the admissions committee get to know you.

Here are some items that contribute to a recommendation letter that makes an impact:

* **Focus on academics and analytical skills.** You do not want a regurgitation of your transcript—the Hawk, the Scout, and the Veteran can see your grades for themselves. But you do want a recommender to discuss your ability to contribute in class and how you are able to think through problems. When presented with a difficult situation, you attempt to solve it.

- ◆ **Give specific examples of events and successes.** What is better than saying you are a great problem solver? Providing the narrative for how you worked your way through a discussion in social studies class last week. Ask your recommenders if, when possible, they can be specific in their letters. Going one step further, when you meet with a teacher to ask for her recommendation letter, have a few moments in mind that you think would be appropriate content for the teacher to use in the letter. You also can mention these when you follow up with the teacher with a note or e-mail after your meeting.

Write stories rather than descriptions. Continuing with the theme of providing specific examples, the best recommendations read like conversations. They do not overdo the assignment and make the applicant sound like a Nobel Prize winner.

———

The most important thing to keep in mind when working toward your teacher recommendations is that there is no such thing as providing too much information to a teacher when you ask for a recommendation letter. Do not worry about appearing pushy. Most teachers deal with more than one hundred students daily. Not only are they unlikely to know much about you outside of class, even if they are more familiar with you, they will appreciate the reminders that you provide instead of having to delve into their memory to see what they can recall about you.

Even if you do come across as overly aggressive, at worst you will be seen as someone who feels strongly about getting admitted to the school of your choice.

The recommendation that Mrs. Day wrote for me certainly made an impact for my chances of admission at NMH. This kid from Texarkana needed every bit of help he could get trying to get into an elite New England prep school after the application deadline. By supplying the pertinent information to Mrs. Day, I helped her craft a recommendation letter that helped the Hawk, the Scout, and the Veteran continue to get to know Whole Ross.

Myth: Writing a recommendation letter is easy for a teacher to do.

Fact: It requires work on their part, but if you meet with them and provide them with a detailed Brag Sheet, you will make things easier for the teachers and get the recommendations you desire.

CHAPTER 10

HOW TO MASTER YOUR INTERVIEW

There is no question what is the most nerve-wracking moment of the entire private or boarding school application process. You are in an unfamiliar place, in an unfamiliar setting, doing something you have never done before. Your hands start to shake. Your voice cracks. The on-campus interview is cause for the most poised of applicants to break into a cold sweat and forget about even the most basic of things.

It is only natural. You are not accustomed to being on these campuses. Even if you are visiting your fifth school and going for your fifth admissions interview, there is only a small chance you are relaxed for such an intimidating event as you sit in an office with the Hawk, the Scout, or the Veteran—all of whom are more than twice your age and do hundreds of these interviews each year where the pressure is squarely on the applicant. There is no such thing as the Hawk, the Scout, or the Veteran having a bad interview.

With this in mind, you should know that interview preparation is one of the most important things you can do in the application process. Although it is impossible to replicate this interview—no matter how good a job the mock interviewer does, you know it is not the real thing—you must prepare properly. Too many applicants fail to do this, and when it comes to game day, they are such a Nervous Nellie that they bomb in the interview and fail to make a positive impression. The admissions process is so competitive—most of the schools on Top Test Prep's top-ten lists admit less than one in five applicants—that you cannot afford to waste this opportunity and be lumped in with the rest of the applicant pool, where most of the students have the same grades and test scores.

In mock interviews, focus on your answers to open-ended questions. These elite schools are getting thousands of applications, so the admissions officers seldom research each applicant they interview ahead of time and develop specific questions for that applicant. The interview is the moment for the Hawk, the Scout, and the Veteran to learn about and get to know the applicant so that her application comes to life and is more than just a series of paper work. Your job, as the applicant, is to forge that personal connection and demonstrate your passion.

Interview tip: When doing mock interviews, focus on presentation. Have a firm—not a wet noodle—handshake to show you mean business. This will make an even bigger impression for girls. Look the interviewer in the eye when greeting them and while speaking throughout the interview; this shows a level of comfort. Sit up straight, and don't slouch in your seat. Be confident—project your voice when speaking, and don't mumble. Pretend that you are speaking to someone standing all the way across the room. These things sound so easy, but they are difficult to master, even for adults, let alone a thirteen-year-old who has never been in such a situation with an unfamiliar adult. I don't care what grade you are in, though; these are things that everyone can do. If you are uncomfortable speaking in public, I recommend a crash course—be it reading a book, watching videos online, or some other method—in learning how to overcome this fear and be comfortable speaking in front of others. This will serve you well in the interview.

Some people will read these recommendations and become robotic in their actions. This is the last thing you want to do. It is critical that your personality comes across and that you comport yourself properly.

Parent tip: This is the opportunity to help your children. These are important details that an admissions officer wants to see. One way to practice these things is to insist your child pay attention to them in all of their dealings for one month leading up to their campus visits and interviews. If your child grows comfortable with doing this in her daily routine, there is a much higher chance your child will continue this behavior in her interview.

———

Now that you are working on how to handle yourself during the interview, let's consider what you should wear to the interview. Boys do not need to wear a tuxedo, and girls do not need a flashy prom dress. For boys, I recommend a blazer and a button-down shirt. If a school requires boys to wear ties to class, then you should wear a tie to your interview—you don't want to be less formal than every boy on campus. Failing to wear a tie in this instance would show that perhaps you would not fit in at the school. Girls, please dress conservatively, but not overconservatively. It does not matter if you wear a dress or pants—go with whichever feels most comfortable.

Myth: You should dress as formally as possible.

Fact: It is appropriate to dress either business casual or similar to the student dress code.

Most important is a neat appearance. If you cannot dress appropriately for an interview when you have your parents' guidance, a boarding school admissions officer will observe, how will you survive on your own? Don't be a wrinkle ball. Make sure your clothes are ironed, your shirt is tucked in, and your socks match. This is stating the obvious, but don't wear sneakers.

Boys, if you are going to wear a tie but do not know how to tie a knot, have your parents help you before you arrive on campus—not in the admissions office or anywhere else on campus where the Hawk, the Scout, the Veteran, or even the student leading you on a campus tour might observe this. Plenty of applicants and even students who have matriculated have difficulty tying their ties, but this remains an obstacle to tackle privately.

> **Interview tip:** Take a deep breath and look around. Since you are well prepared, you know to arrive early at the admissions office. Walk around the room and see if there is anything that looks interesting or something to which you have a connection. Same thing goes for when the Hawk, the Scout, or the Veteran welcome you into the office. If you hope to play lacrosse for the school and see a trophy with a lacrosse player atop it in the Scout's office, don't you think it would make for a strong conversation topic? Of course it would.

If you don't find anything here, feel free to go to the best icebreaker in the world: "Where are you from?" People love to talk about themselves. In turn, this usually leads the interviewer to ask the applicant where she is from and let the applicant talk about her hometown—something the applicant is familiar with and able to talk about at ease.

While it is natural to be nervous, this is not an inquisition or a job interview. At a job interview, the applicant is trying to take the employer's money. At a school interview, the applicant is trying to win the privilege of giving the school money. The dynamics of each interview are quite different.

Also, if you are interviewing at a boarding school, address the admissions officer on a first-name basis. At a private day school, you should be more formal.

During the course of the interview, in addition to answering questions, you should be asking questions of the admissions officer. This reinforces your interest in the school and helps forge that two-way bond you want to achieve. But be careful—under no circumstances should you ask a question that you could have easily looked up on the school website.

- *Do not* ask how many students are in the school.

- *Do not* ask about the average class size.

- *Do not* ask how many students the school annually sends to Harvard.

Instead, convey your interest and smile a lot. Remember, admissions officers are people, too. It is much harder for them to reject an applicant they like. Also make sure the dialogue is a conversation. Yes, you want to be sure to tell the admissions officer all about yourself and let her get to know you, but—much like your personal statement—it should not be "me…me…me." In a conversation in which you are selling yourself, 80 percent should be you asking questions and 20 percent should be how you will use your experience to fulfill these questions.

Myth: Reciting your accomplishments is impressive, and you should list everything you have done during your interview to make certain the admissions officer knows everything about you.

Fact: The interview is your chance to make an impression on the admissions officer, and the best way to do it is by showing your passion for one or two things. Boarding and private school applicants rarely have a long list of authentic accomplishments, so reciting these feats can make you seem like either an egomaniac or someone who lacks true passion. Focus on the things that are important to you, and make sure to drive home this message.

Also, I like to share a story with applicants from my father about his time trying to get into medical school despite continually struggling with chemistry classes. He studied as hard as he could and went to exam reviews. What helped him most from all of this preparation was that he noticed when instructors would pay a lot of attention to one item, as he knew this would be covered on the upcoming test.

How does this pertain to boarding and private school admissions, you ask? There is a direct correlation.

Instead of listening to instructors in exam reviews, listen to the admissions officers. Ask them in a soft, eloquent way, "What do you look for in an applicant?" As soon as you leave the interview, write this down and reference it in your thank-you letter, personal statement, or supplemental essay. Even if an admissions officer sees this as a gratuitous way to make yourself appear to fit in, she will appreciate your interest and memory.

———

After the interview, be sure to follow up with a handwritten thank-you note to the person with whom you interviewed. Yes, it is easier to send this note via e-mail, but using a pen, attaching a stamp on the envelope, and putting the United States Postal Service to work is another demonstration of your interest in gaining admission.

The note can be short, maybe three or four paragraphs. Thank the admissions officer for her time, and convey your desire to attend the school. You might include a picture of yourself so the admissions officer is able to place your face and remember your interview. You should also reference your interview and your campus visit, noting something that you particularly enjoyed. An example follows:

Dear John,

Thank you so much for taking the time for our interview last week. I had a great time on my visit to Hotchkiss and enjoyed getting to know you and the story of how you ended up working at your alma mater. I cannot wait for the fall and hope to be able to join you on campus and try out for the tennis team you coach. The tennis facility is amazing, with so many courts in excellent condition.

Sincerely,

Ross Blankenship

This sample note is short and sweet. It thanks the admissions officer and references the interview and something the applicant and admissions officer have in common. Parents, do not write thank-you notes for your children, and do not write your own thank-you notes.

> **Writing tip:** It is easy to confuse your different campus visits, especially if you make multiple visits on consecutive days, as many applicants do, and you might not write your thank-you note until a few days after your campus visit. In order to maintain an accurate memory of each conversation and campus visit and avoid mixing things up, I recommend taking out a notepad or your cell phone as soon as you get in the car after the interview and jotting down notes from your visit and interview, including the name and title of the admissions officer who interviewed you. Also, ask for a business card from the admissions officer with whom you interview—you want to make sure to spell her name correctly.

Myth: You can overdo it by writing a thank-you note.

Fact: You should write a personalized letter to the admissions officers who interviewed you, which will add to the theme of making a connection and making sure they know you.

———

The on-campus interview is the most stressful part of the application process, with your hopes of getting admitted to the school of your choice boiled down to a thirty-minute meeting with someone you have never met.

But like a piano player getting ready for her first recital, taking things slowly and preparing to the best of your abilities will make this a much simpler event. If you follow my advice and think things through, you will be prepared to master the interview; leave the Hawk, the Scout, and the Veteran with the right impression; and move closer to attending your dream school.

CHAPTER 11

WHAT HAPPENS IF...

If the application process for private and boarding schools felt like a trip to the dentist, the admission interview had to be the part when you were injected with a heavy dose of Novocain in the middle of your mouth, right where the nerves are most sensitive. But now, a short time later—a few months in this case—the numbness has worn off, and you are ready to enjoy what you worked so hard to achieve.

Let's start off with the fun part: What should you do if you are admitted to multiple schools?

If you only get into one school, your options are limited. But if you receive more than one offer of admission, you have a choice to make. There are many ways to figure out where you should enroll.

First, it is likely that during the application process, there was one school that stood out as your top choice among the schools. If you are admitted to this school, send in the deposit to secure your place in the student body, and then notify the other schools that you decline their offer of admission. This is an important courtesy, as it allows those other schools to move forward with plans to fill out their incoming classes. It is much appreciated by those schools, and, you never know, perhaps you might decide to transfer in a year or two—if this is the case, the schools will remember how you handled the situation in a mature manner and will be more inclined to admit you again.

Lacking a clear-cut top choice, there are many variables for you to consider.

- Is one of your options more prestigious than the rest, sending a higher percentage of its graduates to the Ivy League or other top colleges in which you are interested? I know this may sound a bit pompous, but it is something to which you should give strong consideration.

- Was there one school where you felt the best connection to the Hawk, the Scout, or the Veteran—or perhaps the soccer or football coach?

- Do the schools you are considering have similar tuition? Or is one school $5,000 less—$20,000 over the course of a four-year high school career—than the other schools?

- Are the schools you are considering offering comparable financial aid packages? Or is one significantly better than the others?

- Are the schools a similar distance from your home, allowing you to see your parents and siblings more easily? If the schools you are considering are far from home, are they similarly accessible to an airport with flights to your hometown?

- Do the schools have similar facilities or a record of success in a sport that you plan to play?

- Do the schools have a track record of producing a significant number of students who go on to a certain profession in which you are interested, perhaps engineering?

Whatever the case, there will always be metrics to help determine where you should enroll. It is incumbent on you and your parents to look at all of these factors and determine which is most important to you—this list will vary by student.

For instance, when choosing his college, a good friend of mine was deciding between two top liberal arts schools in the Northeast. He was recruited to play tennis at both colleges, which were between a four- to six-hour drive from his home in the Washington suburbs. Academically, the schools were comparable, as were their tuitions and the financial aid packages they were offering. One had a remote rural campus, while the other was located in a city of fifty thousand people. For my friend, the decision came down to his feelings toward the tennis program. While one school had better facilities, with four indoor courts on campus, my friend chose the other school because he had a better relationship with the tennis coach there, even though the team had to drive fifteen minutes from campus and practice at ten at night in order to get indoor court time when it was too cold to play outside. Although this was my friend's college choice, it mirrors the thought process you should have when choosing a boarding or private school.

For instance, remember Julie, the soccer player from California I told you about earlier? The success of the girls' soccer team and her relationship with the girls' soccer coach at each school played significant roles in her desire to attend Lawrenceville.

For some students with whom we have worked, financial aid and cost of tuition were the biggest factors. While all private and boarding schools provide a substantial amount of financial aid each year to defray the high cost of attending these schools, the financial expense remains significant for many. Some families have no problem with this expense, but for others it is a deciding factor. Many students make their school choice because one school is more financially attractive to their parents.

As soon as you start hearing back from the admissions offices, you should create a chart listing each of the schools to which you have been accepted. Rank each of the schools on any factors that are important to you. While you should not feel as though you must adhere to this ranking in choosing your school—it is difficult to weight the factors if one is significantly more important than the others—this will form a guide for you to use in your decision making.

If you are choosing between schools on Top Test Prep's top-ten lists, the decision will be difficult as these schools are all terrific and have so much to offer. While the choice will be tough to make, rest assured that any decision you reach will be the correct one.

Maybe the news was not as rosy for some of you when you went to the mailbox, opened the letter from the school that is your first choice, and found out you were waitlisted. Ugh!

Should you be disappointed? Angry? Just move on to the other schools to which you have been admitted?

While it is acceptable to harbor any of these feelings, it is important to look at the situation matter-of-factly and determine your course of action. Some applicants will be so turned off by not being accepted that they look at being waitlisted as a rejection and no longer want anything to do with a school. Others take a more rational approach and see this as just one more hurdle to clear in order to gain admission. While I understand the first group, it is important to maintain your composure and not react emotionally. This is an important decision that will affect the rest of your life. If you felt so strongly about wanting to attend a school, that feeling should not change by being waitlisted. Yes, it would have been nice simply to have been accepted right off the bat, but being waitlisted still beats being rejected.

So what should you do?

Take note of any schools to which you were admitted and make a list of their enrollment deadlines. The last thing you want to do is be on the waitlist for your top choice, miss out on the other schools, and then not get off the waitlist. You—or, more likely, your parents since they will sign the checks—also would prefer not to send in a deposit check to one of the schools to which you are admitted and have to forfeit that money when you get off the waitlist at your top choice. In this instance your second-choice school will be happy to cash your check, but they will not be happy at losing a prospective student for whom they have reserved a space in their incoming class.

Once you have a timeline in place for when you must reach a decision, call the admissions office of the school that waitlisted you. Ask about the process for getting off the waitlist. Stress that this is your top choice, and if you are admitted, you will enroll. Remember, the Hawk, the Scout, and the Veteran prefer to admit students who feel strongly about attending their school. This holds true for getting off the waitlist as well.

Next, you should be in regular contact with the admissions office, writing a short note each week. The note should not be a nag—*Hey, did I get in yet?*—but rather make each note about yourself. Mention things that you do and how they relate to the school that you want to attend.

> Dear John,
>
> I wanted to let you know that I played the lead role in our school's production of *Romeo and Juliet* this past weekend. It went well, and we had a sold-out auditorium both nights! I can only imagine how much fun it would be to perform in the beautiful arts center on your campus. It would be an honor to have that opportunity. Please let me know if there is anything I can do to help my application.
>
> Sincerely,
>
> Ross

Once again, it is important to be short and sweet. You don't want to force-feed a three-page letter to an admissions officer each week. That is a quick way to have her tune you out. Instead, your notes serve the purpose of making sure the school is aware of your situation and your desire to be admitted there. If a spot opens up in the incoming class, you want to make sure that the Hawk, the Scout, and the Veteran have you in mind.

Myth: If you are waitlisted, that's it. You just wait to hear from the admissions office whether you will be admitted.

Fact: Not all spots on the waitlist are created equal. There are ways to help achieve your goal of getting off the waitlist and into the school of your choice.

———

What about if the envelope you receive in the mail is super skinny, obviously only one page, and containing bad news—the rejection letter that no one wants to receive?

Is there anything you can do?

Not immediately. All of the begging, pleading, cajoling, and arguing is not going to prompt the admissions committee to change its mind. Unfortunately, for whatever reason, you did not meet the criteria for what the admissions officers want in their incoming class. Don't bother calling or writing to ask for an explanation; it will be seen only as whining.

Instead, if this is a school for which you have strong feelings, send the admissions officers a note, thanking them for their consideration. Do you know how few students do this—let alone applicants who were not admitted? It will make an impression. And if you feel strongly about that school, you can always reapply the following year. A show of persistence and a strong desire to attend a school will help your chances of getting admitted.

Myth: No means no. If your application is rejected by a school, you can forget about ever attending that school.

Fact: You can—and should—reapply the following year if a school that you have a strong desire to attend rejects you. The admissions officers will note your persistence and determination.

MY STORY IS YOURS, TOO.

By this point you are ready to take the next step. Whether you are bound for boarding school or a private day school, I hope your journey is as enjoyable and beneficial as mine was. I was a young boy just hitting puberty when I arrived at boarding school, a place that seemed foreign to a fourteen-year-old from Texarkana. My first days at school were challenging, as I had little in common with many of my classmates. Even though I enrolled at NMH and my brother at Exeter, where our personalities were supposed to fit better at each respective school—my wild spirit, his more structured and composed personality—it was still tough, initially.

But things started to click as I forged a bond with my Latin teacher, David Demaine. He kept his home phone number on the dry erase board in the front of his classroom and encouraged his students to use it if we ever needed to—along with a phrase written in Latin, "Salvete, Omnes!"

David was an imposing figure with a stocky build, and he was the school's wrestling coach. But this massive person also was a fatherly figure. And while I certainly had a strong relationship with my father, David filled an important role in my life as I entered boarding school.

More than two thousand miles from Texas, I was quite homesick. David Demaine was the reason I stayed at NMH. I got to know him—and his wife, Gail, a school dean who reprimanded me on occasion—better than anyone, as he created a family environment in and out of the classroom. Because of our relationship, I threw myself into his classes on Latin and classic literature. He was so inspiring that I looked forward each day to learning a dead language—and some of his strategies are now incorporated into Top Test Prep's techniques to prepare for the SSAT, ISEE, SAT,

ACT, MCAT, and many other exams. In fact, David Demaine and another incredible Latin teacher and woman, Jessica Mix Barrington, were there for me through some difficult times. This is the essence of boarding schools: the personalized curricula, a vast amount of extracurricular activities available, and opportunities to explore new worlds—personified through people like David and Jessica.

I feel lucky to have met someone like David Demaine and was incredibly sad to hear that he passed away recently. His teachings will last forever.

In addition to the family environment that David fostered, my four years at NMH were influenced by my participation on the crew team. I was not a natural athlete and did not play a sport as a freshman, but I was struck by how I saw several members of the crew team eating dinner together in the dining hall each night. The rowers were tall, and so was I—and I yearned for the bonds it seemed those teammates had formed. I decided to give the sport a try during my sophomore year.

The first week of practice was rough. I was out of sync with the other rowers. One time I "caught a crab"—where the oar awkwardly caught in the water and flipped back into me, hitting me hard and nearly sending me overboard into the chilly Connecticut River. However, it was only a short amount of time until I learned to keep up with the other rowers in my boat, and soon I considered myself a regular member of the team. I no longer worried about who I would sit with at dinner. I am thankful for an eccentric and wonderfully talented former coach, Charles "Chuck" Hamilton," for putting me in a boat. He taught the fundamentals and essence of rowing, something I would never have experienced growing up in Texas. Though it wasn't until my time at Cornell that I would be considered "decent" at rowing, he challenged our crew every day to be better. And for this, I'm grateful.

From that point forward, even to today, I felt like a key member of the school community. Boarding school remains a critical part of my identity and helped develop who I am today. In fact, NMH is also positively affecting the lives of others in my family: my sister enrolled at NMH, too, and has enjoyed every minute.

From the time you begin thinking about attending boarding or private day school until the day you mail in your acceptance letter and deposit, the application process can seem daunting. There will be moments when you feel on top of the world and you can't wait to get started on this chapter of your life, and other times when you might want to give up. It is important to keep in mind that this is an arduous process, far from simple. At first, many applicants think they can just send in their application and be done, that their test scores, grades, and perhaps being a legacy will guarantee their spot in next year's incoming class at the school of their choosing. By now, though, you know this is not the case. The application process requires thought, energy, and emotional investment. Follow our strategies, and you will be prepared to succeed in these challenging environments.

Now it's your time to find the best boarding school for you—a place where you meet the great teachers, dorm heads, and admissions officers who make you feel at home, even if you're far from your family.

I believe in the power of you. This confidence comes from consulting for thousands of great kids, some underdogs, many born with no excuses but to succeed. Whoever you are, wherever you are, you can get into the best schools, too. It's worth it.

Admit You!

Ross D. Blankenship

Chairman, TopTestPrep.com

(800) 501-7737

BIOGRAPHY

Ross D. Blankenship is a graduate of NMH School, Cornell University, and Washington University School of Law. He is a renowned admissions expert and the founder of two education companies: Top Test Prep and StudyHall. Ross's love of helping students get into the best schools possible began in boarding school where he led tours and advised the admissions office on prospective students. Through Cornell University he began an elite test prep and admission consulting company called Top Test Prep (TopTestPrep.com). The company has grown substantially, now advising students in more than thirty cities and international students in Korea, Japan, China, England, and South America. The company now has more than 360 private tutors and admissions experts worldwide. Ross's mission remains strong: help any child, anywhere in the world, gain admission to the best schools.

Want to get help from Ross's team?

Call (800) 501-7737 or go to http://toptestprep.com/learn-more

Bonus Material for Tutors

TTP's Official Training Manual

Our Mission

To improve scores with highly focused and targeted programs, led by the best tutors in the world.

The strategies and test prep tips below will help you teach others how to prepare for exams like the SSAT, ISEE, and even later exams, such as the SAT and ACT.

The Structure of Our Programs

1. **Diagnostic**
    Use a real exam—it works best. We use real practice exams and always recommend you do, too, for the most accurate assessment. Most guidebooks are just interpretations of real problems. We want a student to practice in the exact conditions and with actual test questions.
2. **Tutor Pairing**
    We pair our students with tutors who are graduates to top schools, and most often, to the schools to which a student is aiming to gain admission.
3. **Briefing**
    We brief the chosen tutor about the student's greatest needs. However, this doesn't mean you should just focus on weak spots. Each tutor will have the ability to customize her student's lessons based on the diagnostics that the tutor grades and the immediate feedback the tutor gets during lesson time.
4. **Program Monitoring**
    We monitor every program to ensure quality. How? Every week, we analyze the student's practice exams and make a candid assessment of the program. If you're training to be a tutor or helping someone prepare for these exams—once a week is a great starting point to measure quality.
5. **Efficacy and Evaluation**
    We like to make sure the tutoring program went flawlessly. After a student takes an exam, call them within twenty-four hours, and ask how the exam was, what they

can recall, and how they think they did overall. If you're working with Top Test Prep, you'll also be able to see your survey results, and the questionnaire provided to the family, after the program and exam are completed.

HOW TO TEACH MATH

Math is universal. Math is a language that transcends all cultural boundaries and pervades our human culture, and yet, there is a prevalent and transcendent fear among students that math is harder than any other subject.

Two core things need to be done to improve a student's math abilities: (1) instill confidence in students, and prove to them that math isn't that bad, and (2) give them key methods that provide a solid foundation for any math they approach.

Core Top Test Prep Math Methods

Confidence Plus Strategy

(1) Build confidence by starting with harder questions.

The key to building a confident math student is to always start with harder questions. In any math section, you should begin by working through the most difficult problems and working backward to the easier problems. After working through the fundamentals of what students know in a "hard" problem, you can then work through the easier problems faster and more efficiently.

When a student begins with some doubts about her math abilities because of these hard problems, it will make the easy- and medium-level-difficulty problems seem much easier. That is the goal! On most standardized exams and subject tests, between 75 and 80 percent of the questions are considered easy to medium difficulty by random test takers.

(2) Here is one of Top Test Prep's key math strategies.

Unwrap!

Step 1: **Underline** the prompt (i.e., the question that's being asked)

Step 2: **Write** the relevant formulas and equation next to the problem.

Step 3: **Assemble** the equation.

Step 4: **Plug** the numbers and solve…and always double-check your answer!

This basic acronym has worked for numerous students who Top Test Prep has helped improve their math scores. Try it out, and see if it works!

Improving math skills takes time, but if you can employ this method you will see results with your students.

HOW TO TEACH READING

We're not trying to teach students how to read for the first time. Rather, we're trying to teach students how to become *active* instead of *passive* readers. Many schools teach students to simply read a book and then write a report after they're done reading. The problem with this basic approach is that it forces students to be passive 99 percent of the time (i.e., when they were actually reading the passage) and to only spend 1 percent of the time actually processing and handling the words and passages contained within as they write their report. There are two key methods that allow students to become better at attacking standardized reading passages: (1) take active and insightful notes on passages, and (2) become the author of the text or passage.

Top Test Prep Reading Methods
    The Student as the Author

(1) Take active and insightful notes looking for *tone and point of view.*

The key to taking active and insightful notes is to look at the passages differently from how you're taught in school. The test makers want you to get lost in the details and in the miscellaneous, superfluous information. Perhaps the test makers have chosen an obscure passage or topic that you've never heard of in all of your schooling. No matter the topic, you must analyze the passage with vigor, looking for tone and point of view. These are the cruxes of all standardized test questions.

Your notes should include (a.) circled keywords that indicate an author's point of view, and (b.) notes in the margins that describe what you think the author's point of view and tone actually is. Keep these "in the margin notes" to three or four words max. It will save you time and also serve as a mnemonic when you begin to answer the passage questions.

*Note we don't think that reading the questions first before reading the passage is an effective tool to answer the questions. This faulty strategy employed by most test prep companies causes students to miss the "big picture" that is gleaned from the tone and point of view.

Instead, try the **Top Test Prep "TAP" Method:**

A. **Title**. Write your own title. Students should be able to add their own creative title to the top of any passage so as to better understand the author's point of view. Most reading passages have italicized summaries at the head of each passage—replace this with a four- to five-word clever title.

B. **Annotate**. You should add important notes and mnemonics in the side margin of the passage. This will help prepare you for the questions that follow.

C. **Point of View**. At the end of any passage, write a two-sentence description describing the purpose of the passage. This will provide a better foundation for attacking the reading questions.

(2) The student must **become the author**.

Part of Top Test Prep's belief in how students become better readers is that they should be able to add their own title to any passage. By doing this and by being able to explain why they titled the passage as such, the student exemplifies a deeper understanding. They then become the author themselves, and everyone knows the author is the best to answer questions about her subjects, topics, and beliefs.

HOW TO TEACH WRITING

There are *three things* that students can do to become better writers for standardized tests: (1) organize their thoughts and thesis, (2) support their assertive point of view with strong evidence, and (3) make their essay flow logically with natural transitions and conclusions.

Top Test Prep Writing Methods: Organize, Support, and Flow

(1) Organization is everything.

When students read an excerpt at the beginning of a standardized test and then are given an assignment, they often panic because they are given so little "information" to work with. The excerpt given might be no more than two to three sentences, and the assignment might be nothing more than an imperative such as, "Explain…" or "Develop your point of view." The key is to structure your outline around your own point of view. The point of view must be assertive! Take a stance, and don't be shy! Be neither passive in your point of view (thesis) nor flippant. From this firm point of view and introduction, you should organize a solid essay that has at least two paragraphs with supporting evidence.

The organization and appearance of an *excellent essay* is as follows:

A. Introduction with a strong thesis and point of view

B. Two to three paragraphs with supporting evidence (**and counterexample[s] if time permits*)

C. Conclusion with a recap of evidence and point of view

(2) Support your point of view with **strong evidence**.

The test makers and graders aren't evaluating whether your thesis or point of view is correct; the graders are looking to see if you can support your thesis with cogent and relevant evidence. Don't worry about what the graders think of you. Spend time instead giving evidence to make them believe your argument, and then give counterevidence to show that you understand both sides of the argument.

For example, if you believe that the United States government should spend more money on space exploration with NASA, you should include at least two to three examples of something like what NASA has done to help our country. Or if you believe that the length of the school year should be shortened, you could write a strong introduction declaring the faults of a longer school year, and then support this thesis with two paragraphs that show what students could learn outside of the school during their free time. However, be prepared to give counterexamples, such as what some students might do in their free time (i.e., probably watch TV and play video games).

(3) Flow logically with **natural transitions**. (Read the essay out loud!)

Most students spend time writing as much as possible without keeping in mind that each paragraph must flow naturally from its preceding paragraph. In the original outline of the essay, the introduction should lead to the first supporting paragraph, which should then strengthen the next paragraph, and so on until the essay's recapping conclusion. If there is an abrupt discussion or non sequitur which doesn't flow naturally, the grader will know, and the student will lose points. If possible, students should read the essay out loud (note: in class or at home only) to make sure that the essay sounds like what they intended.

HOW TO TEACH VOCABULARY

Yes, vocabulary can be taught. It's not just a process of memorization that allows students to understand words. In fact, there are **three levels to vocabulary building**.

(1) Memorization and categorization

(2) Use of words in daily life

(3) Distinguishing and seeing the nuances

Your goal as an instructor is to get students to levels two and three, where students can begin to use the words they learn in their private tutoring and course instruction and then distinguish them by their parts of speech and proper diction. Again, we want students to be *active* learners, making notes on a daily basis about new words they see and applying what they learn in class to the proverbial "real world." Though most lessons and in-home instruction plans are at a maximum six to eight weeks, all students should learn between 15 and 20 new words per week. This will yield between 150 and 200 new words from any given program.

However, because students learn synonyms and antonyms from these original words, they're more likely to learn upward to 500 to 750 new words from their Top Test Prep program. And the best way to learn vocabulary is from the process of "categorizing."

Top Test Prep Vocabulary Prep

Building Categories and Flashcards

Every student should write between fifteen and twenty new flashcards each week. Each of these flashcards should be on jumbo or regular-sized index cards. On the front of the card should be the word itself and its role in the English language (i.e., noun, verb, adjective, or adverb). Once these flashcards are written, they should be placed in a box according to their categorical meaning. If they see a row of words that mean "rich," they should have a category called "wealth" with words like affluent, opulent, lavish, philanthropic, prosperous, and so on. Our brain thinks in terms of categories, and so it is only natural for us to build vocabulary from categorization through these flashcards. Also, use our most-tested words, which you can locate at TopTestPrep.com

Mr. Socrates "The Greek"

Definition of "Socratic Method" at Top Test Prep

- We define it as **interactive discourse, inquiry, and dialogue** that engages students directly and requires that students are prepared at all times.

- All instructors must **know each student's name** and begin questions with the student's name to personalize the course and keep the student on her feet.

- All instructors must "stay on" a student **instead of passing to the next student** so as to not let the student get away with her lack of understanding.

- All instructors should **never ask questions sequentially** and must keep questions directed at students in random order.

- All instructors should walk the room and keep students actively participating.

Top Test Prep's Keys to the Socratic Method

(1) Keep students active and prepared at all times.

(2) Know your students.

(3) Ask specific questions—and **begin questions with the students' names**.

The Six Best Tips to Prepare for Any Exam

(1) *Practice sections:* Always take practice sections and exams under "testing conditions." Testing conditions refers to taking an exam during the same time and general day you are scheduled for the actual exam (e.g., Saturdays at nine in the morning).

(2) *The back of the book:* Do not simply look to the back of the book for answers. This causes you to rely on the book and others' knowledge more than your own. Always try the problems first, and then rely on the back of the book to "check" your answer.

(3) *Speed exam taking:* If the student has difficulties with time or time pressures, have the student take the sections under faster time settings. For example, have the student take what would normally be a thirty-minute section in fifteen minutes instead. Like running with weights attached to your ankles, this will make the tests and each section faster for the student.

(4) *Math Problems:* The method is more important than the result. If a student cannot explain how she got to the correct answer, the student won't be able to do it correctly on her own exam. Like any mathematical proof, you want to make sure you have every step down perfectly.

(5) *Verbal Problems:* One method that has worked for Top Test Prep is to have every student read the verbal passages out loud before answering the questions. Most test prep companies recommend reading the questions first and then skimming the content. During your tutoring sessions, we want the students to hear what the author is writing and then to explain the passage's main point to the tutor. If a student can explain what an author intended to write, the student will know the answers before she gets to the questions. If a student can come up with her own title to the passage, the student becomes more involved and will understand the questions better.

Be sure to make the student the author of the passage.

(6) *On test day*: The Five Ps of Test Prep are simple: Proper preparation prevents poor performance. Make sure students have everything they need on test day: number-two pencils, calculators, and admissions ticket. Being prepared will prevent nervousness and overall anxiety. Students are encouraged to have some caffeine, but not too much. A little caffeine can actually improve a student's performance.

OFFICIAL 365 MOST FREQUENTLY TESTED VOCAB WORDS

You need to know this master list. You can find the definitions on our website, TopTestPrep.com. Memorize, use, and begin distinguishing these words.

A

Abdicate (verb) _____

Aberration (noun) _____

Abject (adj.) _____

Abolish (verb) _____

Abridge (verb) _____

Abstemious (adj.) _____

Accent (verb) _____

Accolade (noun) _____

Acquiesce (verb) _____

Acrimonious (adj.) _____

Acumen (noun) _____

Affable (adj.) _____

Affirmation (noun) _____

Alacrity (noun) _____

Alleviate (verb) _____

Aloof (adj.) _____

Amass (verb) _____

Ambiguous (adj.) _____

Ambivalence (noun) _____

Ambulatory (adj.) _____

Ameliorate (verb) _____

Amity (noun) _____

Anchor (noun) _____

Anchor (verb) _____

Antagonize (verb) _____

Antediluvian (adj.) _____

Antediluvian (noun) _____

Apathy (noun) _____

Apocryphal (adj.) _____

Arcane (adj.) _____

Ascendancy (noun) _____

Atrophy (noun) _____

Augment (verb) _____

Avuncular (adj.) _____

B

Bane (noun) _____

Belie (verb) _____

Belittle (verb) _____

Bellicose (adj.) _____

Belligerence (noun) _____

Benign (adj.) _____

Bizarre (adj.) _____

Blatant (adj.) _____

Blunder (noun) _____

Brevity (noun) _____

Bucolic (adj.) _____

Bucolic (noun) _____

Bungle (verb) _____

Bungle (noun) _____

Burgeon (verb) _____

C

Cajole (verb) _____

Callous (verb) _____

Callous (adj.)_____

Candid (adj.)_____

Cantankerous (adj.) _____

Capitulate (verb) _____

Capricious (adj.)_____

Censure (noun) _____

Censure (verb) _____

Chagrin (noun) _____

Chagrin (verb) _____

Charlatan (noun) _____

Chicanery (noun)_____

Churlish (adj.) _____

Clairvoyant (noun)_____

Clairvoyant (adj.) _____

Clemency (noun) _____

Coalesce (verb)_____

Cohere (verb) _____

Complacent (adj.) _____

Compress (verb) _____

Compress (noun) _____

Confide (verb) _____

Confound (verb) _____

Congeal (verb) _____

Congenial (adj.) _____

Contaminant (noun) _____

Converge (verb) _____

Convivial (adj.) _____

Copious (adj.) _____

Corroborate (verb)_____

Corrugated (adj.) _____

Corrupt (verb) _____

Corrupt (adj.) _____

Cowardice (noun) _____

Credence (noun) _____

Cryptic (adj.)_____

Cupidity (noun) _____

Cursory (adj.) _____

D

Daunt (verb) _____

Dauntless (adj.)_____

Debilitate (verb) _____

Decorous (adj.)_____

Delusion (noun)_____

Deplete (verb)_____

Derelict (adj.) _____

Deviate (verb) _____

Dictum (noun) _____

Didactic (adj.)_____

Discrepancy (noun) _____

Disdain (noun) _____

Disdain (verb)_____

Disentangle (verb) _____

Disingenuous (adj.) _____

Distend (verb)_____

Docile (adj.) _____

Drawback (noun) _____

Dubious (adj.) _____

E

Edict (noun) _____

Efface (verb) _____

Effervescent (adj.) _____

Eloquent (adj.) _____

Enhance (verb) _____

Enigmatic (adj.) _____

Entourage (noun) _____

Ephemeral (adj.) _____

Ephemeral (noun) _____

Epitome (noun) _____

Equilibrium (noun) _____

Equivocate (verb) _____

Erudite (adj.) _____

Eschew (verb) _____

Eulogy (noun) _____

Euphonious (adj.) _____

Evacuate (verb) _____

Evanescent (adj.) _____

Exacerbate (verb) _____

Exclude (verb) _____

Exculpate (verb) _____

Expedite (verb) _____

Expendable (adj.) _____

Extol (verb) _____

F

Facilitate (verb) _____

Fallow (noun) _____

Fallow (adj.) _____

Famished (adj.) _____

Fastidious (adj.) _____

Fathom (noun) _____

Fathom (verb) _____

Fertile (adj.) _____

Fidelity (noun) _____

Flourish (verb) _____

Foible (noun) _____

Foster (verb) _____

Fraudulent (adj.) _____

Frugal (adj.) _____

Fruitful (adj.) _____

Fruitless (adj.) _____

Furtive (adj.) _____

Futile (adj.) _____

G

Garner (verb) _____

Garner (noun) _____

Gaudy (adj.) _____

Generic (noun) _____

Generic (adj.) _____

Genre (noun) _____

Germane (adj.) _____

Glean (verb) _____

Glib (adj.) _____

Gluttony (noun) _____

Grandiose (adj.) _____

Gratuitous (adj.) _____

Gregarious (adj.) _____

Grotto (noun) _____

Guile (noun) _____

Gullible (adj.) _____

Gusto (noun) _____

H

Hackneyed (adj.) _____

Harbinger (noun) _____

Harbinger (verb) _____

Haughty (adj.) _____

Hefty (adj.) _____

Hiatus (noun) _____

Hideous (adj.) _____

Hilarity (noun) _____

Hinder (verb) _____

Hone (verb) _____

Humane (adj.) _____

Husbandry (noun) _____

Hybrid (noun) _____

Hyperbole (noun) _____

Hypocritical (adj.) _____

I

Iconoclast (noun) _____

Idiosyncratic (adj.) _____

Imperial (adj.) _____

Impudent (adj.) _____

Inchoate (adj.) _____

Incite (verb) _____

Inconspicuous (adj.) _____

Incorrigible (adj.) _____

Indignant (adj.) _____

Indolent (adj.) _____

Ineffable (adj.) _____

Innocuous (adj.) _____

Insolent (adj.) _____

Invocation (noun) _____

Irascible (adj.) _____

Ironic (adj.) _____

Irrefutable (adj.) _____

J

Jargon (noun) _____

Jeopardize (verb) _____

Jettison (verb) _____

Jocular (adj.) _____

Jocular (adv.) _____

Judicious (adj.) _____

Juxtapose (verb) _____

K

Kindle (verb) _____

Kinetic (adj.) _____

Kudos (noun) _____

L

Lackadaisical (adj.) _____

Laconic (adj.) _____

Languid (adj.) _____

Laud (verb) _____

Lax (adj.) _____

Leniency (noun) _____

Levitate (verb) _____

Levity (noun) _____

Listless (adj.) _____

Loquacious (adj.) _____

Lucid (adj.) _____

Lugubrious (adj.) _____

M

Magnanimous (adj.) _____

Maladroit (adj.) _____

Malleable (adj.) _____

Maxim (noun) _____

Mellifluous (adj.) _____

Mendacious (adj.) _____

Mendicant (noun) _____

Mercurial (adj.) _____

Mettle (noun) _____

Misanthrope (noun) _____

Miscreant (noun) _____

Mitigate (verb) _____

Mobile (adj.) _____

Mollify (verb) _____

Morbid (adj.) _____

Motley (verb) _____

Motley (adj.) _____

Mundane (adj.) _____

Munificent (adj.) _____

Myopic (adj.) _____

Myriad (noun) _____

Myriad (adj.) _____

N

Nadir (noun) _____

Narcissistic (adj.) _____

Nebulous (adj.)_____

Nefarious (adj.) _____

Negligible (adj.) _____

Nepotism (noun) _____

Nexus (noun) _____

Nomad (noun) _____

Nonchalant (adj.)_____

Nostalgia (noun) _____

Nullify (verb)_____

O

Obdurate (adj.) _____

Oblivion (noun) _____

Obscure (verb) _____

Obscure (adj.)_____

Obsequious (adj.)_____

Obtuse (adj.)_____

Odyssey (noun)_____

Onerous (adj.) _____

Onus (noun) _____

Opacity (noun) _____

Opaque (adj.) _____

Opulent (adj.)_____

Oscillate (verb) _____

Ostentatious (adj.) _____

Overt (adj.) _____

P

Pacify (verb) _____

Palpable (adj.) _____

Panacea (noun) _____

Pander (verb) _____

Parity (noun) _____

Parsimony (noun) _____

Patent (noun)_____

Patent (verb)_____

Patent (adj.) _____

Paucity (noun) _____

Pedantic (adj.) _____

Pejorative (adj.) _____

Penchant (noun) _____

Penury (noun) _____

Perfidy (noun) _____

Perfunctory (adj.) _____

Peripatetic (adj.) _____

Peripheral (adj.) _____

Petulant (adj.) _____

Pilfer (verb) _____

Placate (verb) _____

Placid (adj.) _____

Precise (adj.) _____

Premeditated (adj.) _____

Pretentious (adj.) _____

Prevalent (adj.) _____

Probity (noun) _____

Proclivity (noun) _____

Prodigal (noun) _____

Prodigal (adj.) _____

Prodigious (adj.) _____

Profuse (adj.) _____

Provoke (verb) _____

Proximity (noun) _____

Prudence (noun) _____

Puerile (adj.) _____

Pugnacious (adj.) _____

Pulverize (verb) _____

Q

Quagmire (noun) _____

Queasy (adj.) _____

Querulous (adj.) _____

Quip (noun) _____

Quip (verb) _____

Quirk (noun) _____

Quirk (verb) _____

Quixotic (adj.) _____

R

Rant (verb) _____

Rant (noun) _____

Recalcitrant (adj.) _____

Recant (verb) _____

Reciprocal (adj.)_____

Reclusive (adj.) _____

Remedy (noun) _____

Remedy (verb) _____

Replete (verb)_____

Replete (adj.) _____

Rescind (verb) _____

Reserve (noun)_____

Resolute (adj.) _____

Respite (noun) _____

Rhetoric (noun) _____

Ruffle (verb) _____

Rupture (noun) _____

S

Saccharine (adj.) _____

Salubrious (adj.) _____

Sardonic (adj.) _____

Scrutinize (verb) _____

Seditious (adj.) _____

Sedulous (adj.) _____

Skepticism (noun) _____

Somber (adj.) _____

Sovereign (noun) _____

Sovereign (adj.) _____

Sparse (adj.) _____

Specify (verb) _____

Spontaneous (adj.) _____

Spurn (verb) _____

Squander (verb) _____

Stimulus (noun) _____

Stringent (adj.) _____

Stymie (noun) _____

Stymie (verb) _____

Subtle (adj.) _____

Succinct (adj.) _____

Summary (noun) _____

Summon (verb) _____

Sumptuous (adj.) _____

Sycophant (noun) _____

Symbiotic (adj.) _____

T

Taciturn (adj.) _____

Tangent (noun) _____

Tantamount (adj.) _____

Tawdry (adj.) _____

Tenacious (adj.) _____

Tenuous (adj.) _____

Tranquil (adj.) _____

Transient (noun) _____

Truculence (noun) _____

Truncate (verb) _____

Turbulence (noun) _____

U

Ubiquitous (adj.) _____

Urbane (adj.) _____

Usurp (verb) _____

V

Venality (noun) _____

Venerable (adj.) _____

Venturesome (adj.) _____

Verbose (adj.) _____

Vex (verb) _____

Viable (adj.) _____

Vibrancy (noun) _____

Vilification (noun) _____

Virulence (noun) _____

W

Wane (verb) _____

Wanton (noun) _____

Wanton (verb) _____

Wary (adj.) _____

Whet (verb) _____

Whittle (verb) _____

Willful (adj.) _____

Wily (adj.) _____

Wont (noun) _____

Z

Zany (noun) _____

Zealot (noun) _____

Zenith (noun) _____

Zephyr (noun) _____

Zest (verb) _____

Zest (noun) _____

Made in the USA
Middletown, DE
12 June 2018